The Critical Thinker

The Path To Better Problem Solving, Accurate Decision Making, and Self-Disciplined Thinking

By Steven Schuster

steveschusterbooks@gmail.com

Copyright © 2018 by Steven Schuster. All rights reserved.

No part of this publication may be reproduced, stored in a retrieval system, or transmitted in any form or by any means, electronic, mechanical, photocopying, recording, scanning or otherwise, except as permitted under Section 107 or 108 of the 1976 United States Copyright Act, without the prior written permission of the author.

Limit of Liability/ Disclaimer of Warranty: The author makes no representations or warranties with respect to the accuracy or completeness of the contents of this work and specifically disclaims all warranties, including without limitation warranties of fitness for a particular purpose. No warranty may be created or extended by sales or promotional materials. The advice and recipes contained herein may not be suitable for everyone. This work is sold with the understanding that the author is not engaged in rendering medical, legal or other professional advice or services. If professional assistance is required, the services of a competent professional person should be sought. The author shall not be liable for damages arising herefrom. The fact that an individual, organization of website is referred to in this work as a citation and/or potential source of further information does not mean that the author endorses the information the individual, organization to website may provide or recommendations they/it may make. Further, readers should be aware that Internet websites listed in this work might have changed or disappeared between when this work was written and when it is read.

For general information on the products and services or to obtain technical support, please contact the author.

Table of Contents

Chapter 1: What is Critical Thinking? 9

Chapter 2: What are the main guidelines of critical thinking? 19

Chapter 3: Piaget's Theory on Thinking 47

Chapter 4: The Science of Paul-Elder 67

Chapter 5: Understand Deeply 95

Chapter 6: How To Develop Critical Thinking Skills 111

Chapter 7: Barriers to Critical Thinking 125

Chapter 8: On Ethics and Impartiality 139

Conclusion 147

Reference 151

Endnotes 159

Chapter 1: What is Critical Thinking?

There is a fable that begins with a man and his horse. The man only had one horse, and the horse ran away. Immediately, his friends began to express their sympathy to him in his time of misfortune, but the man simply responded with a "let's wait and see" attitude for what might be in store for him in the future.

After a few days, the man's horse returned home and had 20 wild horses following him. Again, his friends reacted quickly, ready to celebrate his good fortune, but the man kept his same steady "let's wait and see" perspective.

It wasn't long before the man's luck changed for the worse when one of the wild horses kicked his only son and broke both of his legs. The man's friends rushed to console him, but he continued to just want to "wait and see" what would happen next.

The country went to war, causing all of the young men to be drafted and ultimately killed in battle, but because of his broken legs, the man's son wasn't drafted and his life was spared. The man's friends expressed their joy and gratitude that his son was safe and alive. The man still held on to his "wait and see" outlook on life.[i]

This fable is a good demonstration of critical thinking at work. The man with his calm demeanor despite whatever life brought his way showed that he was a great critical thinker. He never rushed to judgment. He could have easily been consumed or overwhelmed by his feelings so many times, but he chose a logical approach rather than an emotional one. He was always quietly contemplative. Despite any internal questions he may have had or what people around him were thinking and doing, he continued to be a steady and slow thinker. He never gave in to the impulse of being swayed or overly influenced by momentary success or failure. He knew that life would be filled with highs and lows, and he stayed level-headed and even-keeled, come what may.

The Basics of Critical Thinking

Critical thinking is not a new term, and it is one we encounter frequently, especially if we are in the self-help or psychology section of the bookstore. Despite hearing these words on such a regular basis, few of us have probably ever stopped to think about what they mean or given any thought to how we could use critical thinking to our benefit.

Critical thinking occurs when we ask ourselves (and others) questions like "How do you know that?" or "How did you reach that conclusion?" or "What evidence supports this theory?" or "Are there any other possible explanations or alternatives that haven't been considered yet?"

Critical thinkers rarely follow a gut feeling. They use logic and reasoning to reach their conclusions, rather than letting themselves be guided by their emotions. They want evidence to support ideas and don't just accept things at face value. They question things and dig deeper, instead of just accepting things as true because someone said them.

There are three basic characteristics that good critical thinkers have. People who want to incorporate more critical thinking in their lives can benefit from trying to improve these skills:

- **a greater sense of curiosity**
  When people lack curiosity, they are willing to accept the opinions of others as fact without digging deeper and questioning them. They are content to take the easy way out instead of looking for information and trying to learn more. That is the opposite of thinking critically. Good critical thinkers are open-minded and willing to accept the new evidence that they find, rather than just clinging to old beliefs.

- **a healthy dose of skepticism**
  Being skeptical doesn't mean that you say no to or deny everything. It means that you approach new or unproven information with a questioning frame of mind until you learn more. Critical thinkers look for proof or evidence, rather than immediately accepting things. Without a healthy dose of skepticism, it is impossible to be a critical thinker.

- **a humble attitude**

> Good critical thinkers are willing to admit they were wrong when faced with new information. They do not blindly cling to their own opinions. They realize they are humans, and as such, are likely to make mistakes. They accept new evidence and allow it to shape their judgment and thinking.[ii]

If you are ready, willing, and able to ask questions and use the information you learn to guide you toward judgments based on reason rather than emotion, you are ready to become a critical thinker who won't accept ideas as truth without sufficient quality proof to back them up.

Creative Critical Thinking

You may be concerned that critical thinking is very regimented and would stifle creativity, but this simply isn't the case. Thinking critically will actually challenge you to think more creatively because you will need to come up with possible explanations and solutions to problems. Critical thinking and creativity go hand in hand. Your critical thinking makes you question ideas, and then your creative thinking tries to find connections or figure out the big picture of what it all might mean.

In the 1980s, there was a "Critical Thinking Movement" where a major focus in education was in getting children to be critical thinkers in school. This movement believed that there was more to learning than just the rote memorization of facts and content that often felt disjointed and irrelevant to the students. It supported the idea that real learning takes place when the students can roll up their sleeves and discover information for themselves. It was no longer enough for students to be sponges absorbing knowledge presented to them by the teacher. They were expected to develop and strengthen critical thinking skills by questioning things and thinking through problems for themselves. Teachers had to teach and model critical thinking skills for their students so that they could be active participants in their own learning. By taking ownership of their learning, the critical thinking movement believed that they would be more likely to remember what they learned for the long-term, while at the same time strengthening skills that would be valued by their future employers and prove invaluable to them in all areas of their lives. This movement did not stop in the 1980s. In fact, even in the 21st

century, teachers as well as business and political leaders still identify critical thinking as an essential skill that students need to develop to be successful in the workplace and in life. It remains a major driving force in education today, and will most likely be for the foreseeable future.[iii]

Critical thinkers are self-disciplined. They direct their own thinking and use the information they learn to monitor and correct themselves when necessary. Critical thinkers are in control of their own learning and as a result they often come to have a greater understanding of and empathy for differing viewpoints. Who couldn't use a little more of that in their life?

Benefits of Critical Thinking

Critical thinking obviously takes extra time and effort on your part. So you might be asking yourself, "What's in it for me?" Critical thinking may not be easy, but it is so worth it. People who have strong critical thinking skills can do many things that the average person can't. These skills will serve them well in all areas of their lives.

They can see connections between ideas that others may miss. Critical thinkers are able to evaluate and assess theories and ideas to determine their overall importance. Since they refuse to accept things at face value without proof, they are readily able to recognize quality arguments supported by evidence and even create their own to defend their point of view to others. Critical thinkers can find errors in other people's reasoning. They look at problems and approach them logically in a measured step-by-step manner.

How do you know if you are a strong critical thinker? Ask yourself the following questions:

- Are you willing to consider other opinions and possible solutions?
- Are you curious about a variety of topics?
- Do you enjoy learning new things and consider yourself to be a lifelong learner?
- Are you confident in your reasoning skills?
- Is it easy for you to spot times when it is important to put your critical thinking to use?
- Are you willing to wait to pass judgment until you have all the necessary facts?
- Do you keep an open mind when it comes to differing viewpoints?
- Are you understanding of others' ideas and opinions?

- Do you try to be fair and impartial when assessing evidence?
- Are you aware of and honest about their biases, stereotypical thinking, and prejudices so that you don't let them sway your thinking?
- Are you willing to go where the facts take you and change or abandon your previously held opinions when presented with new evidence that warrants the change?

If you can honestly answer yes to those questions most days, then you just might be exhibiting the characteristics of a critical thinker. This book is designed to give you practical advice that you can start putting to work in your life immediately. If you are willing to put forth the time and effort to put that advice into practice, and always strive to keep learning and improving, you just might be surprised at what a strong critical thinker you can become, and all of the many beneficial impacts that may have on your life.

Key Takeaways:

- Critical thinking is a commitment to letting logic and reasoning be the driving force in guiding your judgments and decision-making, rather than giving in to emotion.

- Critical thinkers aren't satisfied without evidence and proof to support ideas and opinions. They are always on a quest for new information, and they are willing to change or abandon previously held beliefs in the face of new, quality evidence.

- Critical thinkers are aware that everyone carries biases and prejudices with them that they must overcome, but they are open-minded about viewpoints that are different from theirs.

- Critical thinking is slow and steady thinking that resists the temptation to give in to impulse or rush to judgment. It requires a sense of curiosity, a healthy dose of skepticism, and a level of humility.

Chapter 2: What are the main guidelines of critical thinking?

Carole Wade and Carol Tavris in their books *Psychology,* (5th Edition, Longman Publishers, 1998), and *Psychology in Perspective*, (2nd Edition, Longman Publishers, 1997), identified seven main aspects of critical thinking. In this chapter, we will take a closer look at these seven main guidelines of critical thinking and how we can apply them to our daily lives.

1. The first step to start thinking critically is learning to ask questions.

Allow your mind to wonder, reflect on your questions, and pay close attention to the answers you get. Try to think of questions that haven't been answered yet. Try to find the areas of a problem or theory that no one has asked questions about. Then ask yourself:

- Why was this part of the problem or theory previously ignored?
- How did we end up where we are?
- What's wrong here?
- Why is this the way it is instead of another way?[iv]

Consider this: People often make changes in their lives, sometimes major ones, based on a single anecdote they have heard from someone. From the restaurants we eat at, to the cars we drive, to the school we enroll our kids in, we often make decisions based on an anecdote or story we hear from someone about their experience with the topic at hand.

A story:

My wife is a brilliant woman—far smarter than I could ever hope to be. Despite her superhero status in our family, she too is human, which means even she is susceptible to this trap. One of my colleagues at work had lost a significant amount of weight while following a specific diet plan. While I do not find the same physical flaws in my wife that she finds in herself, I supported her when she wanted to talk to my colleague about the diet plan she used. My wife is so good at getting to the bottom of things that she could easily be an investigator for the FBI, which is why our kids don't stand a chance at hiding the truth from us. Normally, she isn't satisfied until she has triple-checked a set of facts, but on this particular occasion, she was satisfied with just my colleague's anecdotal endorsement of the diet plan. She was so convinced that this plan would be her ticket to success as well that she instantly subscribed to the website, ordered their protein shakes, and bought their meal plan recipes. After a few months and a valiant effort, my wife did not experience the same results as my colleague.

While she was disappointed, my wife understood that my colleague's success could have been attributed to a variety of factors beyond just the diet plan. Perhaps her portion sizes were much lower on the plan than they had been before, maybe she began an exercise regimen when she started the plan, or maybe she had not previously been eating any healthy foods, so she experienced a greater change on the plan. There could be so many variables at play that the exact cause of her success could be quite difficult to pinpoint. In my wife's eagerness to find something that would quickly and easily work for her, she rushed to judgment and attributed the success solely to the diet plan based on one anecdote she'd heard.

This happens to people all the time. People often rush conclusions without real, definitive evidence. Human nature wants us to find cause and effect relationships, which often hampers critical thinking.

2. Articulate the questions right to define the problem.[v]

The questions you ask are very important, and may make all the difference as to the answers you will find. An inadequately worded question can easily lead to answers that are partial or misleading. It is human nature to not want to be proven wrong, so it is helpful to word your questions in a way that comes across as neutral rather than accusatory. Also, the focus of your questions should be to gather information—not to influence others. If you frame your questions in such a way that it seems you already know the answers, you will be doing yourself a tremendous disservice because you won't get an objective answer.

As you develop your critical thinking skills, it is important to never use them (or the lack of critical thinking skills in other people) to try to make questions that attempt to manipulate the thinking of others to match yours. Manipulation happens when you deliberately frame your question in such a way that you know it will result in a certain answer from another person.

A story:

Companies use this trick in their marketing campaigns all the time. If you have ever watched an infomercial on late night television or the ways goods are promoted on the shopping channels, chances are, you have seen this manipulation at work. The salespeople begin by presenting you with everyday problems they know nearly everyone has—laundry stains, clothing or jewelry concerns, anything that they know a large number of people will be able to relate to. They show you a scenario that you likely experience in your daily life, then ask you questions they can expect the answer to like:

- Does your family get stains on their clothes that are hard to get out?

- Do you wish your detergent would remove every stain the first time you use it?
- Do you feel like you are paying too much for detergent that doesn't deliver consistent quality stain fighting?

Once they have you on track with answering yes to the obvious questions, they will capitalize on your human nature to continue to answer yes and purchase their product. They will attempt to cloud your critical judgment for their financial gain, and it often works. Keeping your critical thinking skills sharp will help you see right through marketing schemes like this.

3. Examine the evidence and look for assumptions and biases.

Think about what evidence validates or disproves the argument you are considering. Don't fall into the common trap of thinking that just because many people believe something, or some people who seem knowledgeable on a topic support the argument, makes it true. Everyone is human, and everyone carries with them their own feelings and biases that affect their ability to be impartial. When you study an argument, consider the biases that others bring to the table in addition to your own.

A story:

Cognitive biases are connected to critical thinking. One of the most common ones is confirmation bias. This is the bias we all harbor within us that makes us think we're always right.

Warren Buffett once said, "What the human being is best at doing is interpreting all new information so that their prior conclusions remain intact." It turns out he is a wise man, because there is science to back up his theory. Our brains are hardwired to look at new information in such a way that it confirms the ideas they already have, instead of trying to disprove or test them. It is human nature to dislike when our ideas and theories are challenged. We tend to automatically try to dismiss things that refute our opinions. It is something we are all guilty of on a regular basis, and we do it without even thinking. The only way we can overcome our cognitive biases is to be aware of them and the role they play in our lives. It is only by recognizing and being attentive to them that we can hope to defeat our biases through questioning.

Why does confirmation bias have such a powerful hold on our brain? Our brains have to sort through so much information and decide what to do with it that it would become overwhelmed if it couldn't take some shortcuts to conserve energy and effort. So why do we tend to think we are right, even when evidence would suggest otherwise? It's just easier. Our brain likes to take the easy path when given a choice. It takes less effort and energy if we get to keep our viewpoints intact, rather than questioning and challenging them to the point where we have to change them.[vi]

We want to become critical thinkers, so we need to rise above the natural tendencies and biases in our brains, like the confirmation bias, in order to find the accurate and objective answers to our questions we are looking for. Critical thinking will not be the quick and easy path our brain prefers to take. I won't tell you that critical thinking is easy, but it is worth it.

Now that you are aware that confirmation bias exists in everyone, you will be able to recognize when it is at work in your own thinking. You know that your human nature will only acknowledge information that supports your ideas and theories, so start practicing actively trying to find information that will disprove them. Practice accepting the thoughts and opinions of others. You may still agree to disagree in the end, but just by acknowledging they exist and that there well may be logical reasoning behind them, you will be improving your critical thinking skills. You will be going a long way toward realizing that there is more than one correct viewpoint in life, and it is entirely possible for there to be many different correct answers and theories coexisting at the same time.

For example, some people have a very strong feeling about cheating. They may be unwilling to ever forgive someone who cheated and have the idea that nothing could ever be done to erase the pain caused by cheating. That is a cognitive bias that may have deep ties to a personal experience and cause such strong emotions to come to the surface. On the other hand, there are many other people who choose to forgive those who have cheated on them and are able to move on and find happiness with their partner again. Being willing to accept that there are people with different opinions and ideas from your own who are able to make them work in their lives is a step toward overcoming confirmation bias.

There will be times you will have to be open to the possibility of many potential solutions and explanations, and other times when you will have to be open to the possibility that there may only be one real answer, and that what you thought was correct may need to be altered once new information is presented. They key is you have to be open-minded and overcome your own confirmation bias to uncover the truth.

4. Emotional reasoning is holding you back.

Always keep in mind that just because you have strong feelings about something doesn't mean it's necessarily right, or that it's right for everyone. People often trust their "gut instinct" completely at the expense of thinking critically or objectively about things first. They are willing to trust their emotions, even when evidence disproves their beliefs. They come to mistake their feelings for facts. They may not recognize that their feelings are tied to one experience in their lives that molded their opinion and may not be rooted in the reality of the present situation at all.

A story:

Have you ever lost a loved one and began to explain some natural occurrences as signs that your loved one was nearby, or even communicating with you? This happens to people quite often in times of grief. They may see things like the shape of a heart in a coffee cup and interpret it as a sign.

I had a similar experience. Shortly after I had lost some family members who I was very close to, I heard the legend that if you see a butterfly and whisper "I love you" as it flies by, it will carry the message to your loved ones in heaven. After I heard that, it seemed that I saw more butterflies than I ever had before. While the logical side of me knew it couldn't actually happen, and I was just more aware of butterflies around me than I had been previously, the emotional side of me still found it a source of comfort during a very difficult time.

There are times when this type of emotional reasoning might prove dangerous. Some people may escape injury from a serious accident and mistakenly assume it means they will be protected from harm in future dangerous situations as well. This may cause them to take unnecessary risks because they think nothing bad will ever happen to them.

Sometimes emotional reasoning takes place just inside our minds. We may have internal thoughts and feelings that happen with or without a basis in fact. Sometimes we may get a gut feeling that something bad is about to happen to ourselves or someone we love. We may not have any evidence to support our theory, but it may make us postpone a trip, avoid a situation, or call to check on those we care about to make sure they are safe. It can result in us feeling very nervous or unsettled until we are absolutely certain that no one is in harm's way.

Even with the pitfalls of emotional reasoning, it is not all bad. When it is combined with and balanced by critical thinking to keep it in check, it can prove helpful to us. Feelings like compassion and empathy for the feelings of others are very important, even as we use our critical thinking to shape our viewpoint. It is never necessary hurt others along the way. There is scientific research to support this. The *Harvard Business Review* recently presented findings from a study which showed that managers who use their intellect in combination with emotional reasoning are more successful than those who rely solely on facts and do not pay any deference to the feelings of others.[vii]

5. Over-generalization is the enemy.

It is important not to stop our thinking process at the basic and obvious level. Too often people try to simplify things to the point of only looking for cause and effect relationships. This causes them to miss the big picture and be closed off to other possibilities. These over-generalizations are definitely obstacles to critical thinking, which seeks to be open and objective in interpreting information, as well as in using it to make reasonable judgments and find potential explanations and solutions to problems.

A story:

Let's see what generalizations are first. Making generalizations involves taking characteristics from a few parts of a group and extending those characteristics to the whole group by nature of association. Generalizing means that we automatically assume the whole group shares the same characteristics after witnessing them in just a few group members.

There are times when making generalizations can prove to be helpful especially in scientific research, as long as it is used properly. It can save valuable time too, if each group member doesn't have to be examined individually and responsible generalizations can be made based on fact. The problem occurs when we make over-generalizations.

For example, I attended a football game at my college alma mater when we played the team we share a fierce rivalry with. There was a group of about five fans from the other team sitting near me. They had been drinking and were behaving in a completely inappropriate and rude manner. If I had assumed that everyone from my university's rival shared the same behavior and characteristics based on the behavior of those five fans, that would have been an over-generalization and very unfair.

What is wrong with a generalization like that? If I based my conclusion about such a large group of people like all of the fans, students, and alumni of the rival university on such a small sample of just five people behaving badly, it would hardly be accurate, objective, or based on fact. I would definitely need a much larger sample size, and observations of them in a variety of situations over time (while overcoming any of my own biases that may be clouding my judgment), before I could even begin to make a fair assessment of the characteristics of the entire group. Even if I expanded my sample size, it may not be enough. I would have to take into account other factors such as age and gender before I could begin to make accurate generalizations about the entire population.

Over-generalizing is the enemy of critical thinking. As we already discussed, our brains look for quick and easy solutions and explanations. They also crave knowledge and certainty. When these two things meet, we get over-generalizations. We make broad judgments based just on a little bit of experience.

Sometimes this can lead us to a biased feeling of negativity about ourselves and our abilities, which can be difficult to overcome. For example, I have always loved to write. I grew up thinking that I had a bit of talent for it and took pride in it based on the grades, comments, and feedback that I received from others. All of that changed in one of my language arts classes in college. Every essay or piece of writing I submitted came back to me with a lot of red ink marking corrections and improvements I needed to make, while it seemed that my classmates were receiving very few on their papers. I took the little information that I received from one professor as an overgeneralization and concluded that I was a terrible writer. I came to dread writing and thought I would never experience success in his class or any other writing experiences in the future. My parents encouraged me to schedule a meeting with my professor to see specifically what areas he thought I really needed to improve and if I could receive any help in honing those skills.

I summoned every ounce of courage I had and met with him. It was during that meeting that he explained to me that he thought I had a gift that had the potential to become a good writer, and he wanted to do his part to help and encourage me. If I had allowed myself to continue to stew in my negativity, I would never have discovered my conclusion was a rush to judgment and was incorrect. I would never have continued to pursue writing and work to improve and develop my craft. My life would have taken quite a different path.

When the limits we place on ourselves through our negativity bias turn into over-generalizations, it can become a very difficult cycle to break. We keep telling ourselves that we can't do things when we actually can. Our brain creates a barrier of our own making that we often fail to break through. We can become insecure and doubt ourselves. We start to avoid situations we think we can't be successful in, and fail to reach our full potential as a result.

So what is the solution to over-generalizations? Thoughtful and deliberate critical thinking can make you objective and much less susceptible to them. The first step is to become more aware of the opinions and thoughts you have about yourself and the world around you. Start looking for areas where you may have already made over-generalizations or kept your thinking too simple. Begin to question that thinking and work to correct it by looking for legitimate proof to substantiate your conclusions.

6. How can a situation be interpreted differently?

Resist the tendency to rush to judgment without enough evidence. Even when you have collected an acceptable amount of quality evidence, ask yourself what other possible explanations there may be before you form your conclusion.

A story:

You may remember back in 2015 when a photo of a dress went viral and was the topic of debate on nearly every daytime talk show and all over social media. Some people looked at the photo and saw a black and blue dress, while others looked at the same photo and saw a gold and white dress. Critical thinking is a lot like this. It doesn't matter what colors people saw in the dress. The point is that they were both looking at the same picture, and both interpretations were correct.

There are times in life when there really is only one correct answer or positive solution to a problem, but even then, it can still be beneficial to hear alternatives presented by others in order to see things from their perspective. It may help you uncover the right answer or best solution, or it may just increase your understanding of and empathy toward others, but in any case, it is worth the time and effort to consider it.

There are other times when we may have to come to the conclusion and accept that there is no right answer, or perhaps even any answer at all. In critical thinking, it is always beneficial to gather as much information as we can from a variety of sources before we come to a conclusion. Being satisfied with incomplete information can easily lead to incomplete or incorrect answers.

For example, have you ever watched very young children playing on the playground? They often approach the slide in vastly different ways. Some run up happily to slides before fearlessly and without hesitation sliding down ones that are quite high, laughing and smiling all of the way. Others will walk up slowly to slides, look, hesitate, and then turn away in fear, refusing to go down even if an adult is holding their hand or waiting to catch them at the bottom. This tells you a lot about the perspective of the children. Those who fear the slide may have had a bad experience where they were hurt on a slide or got scared when they went down faster than they expected, while those who are eager to slide have likely had fun on slides in the past and approach them expecting to experience joy. Technically, both groups of children are correct. Slides can be great fun, but they can also be worthy of caution too as it is possible to get hurt on them. The only problem is both groups of children are relying on partial information to draw their conclusions.

Another bias we have which often stands in the way of our critical thinking is our projection bias. We find it hard to think beyond our own personal experiences and opinions. Projection bias is when we assume everyone's reality is just like ours and so they will think just like we do. This causes to get stuck in our own perspective and not even look for additional information.[viii]

Critical thinking and considering other interpretations is crucial to overcoming this bias. Otherwise, assuming that we are always right can have significant consequences for our lives as we become overconfident in ourselves and our judgments. This is how people can rack up large gambling debts, or mistakenly assume that more people support their ideas than really do.

My mom always told me that two heads are better than one. No matter how smart or accomplished you may be, opening your mind to alternative interpretations, asking questions, and listening to points of view that are different from yours makes you a stronger critical thinker, and likely a more educated human being. Sharing information with and receiving information from others improves your judgment and critical thinking, and increases your knowledge of the world around you.

7. Learn to tolerate uncertainty.

As you develop your critical thinking skills, you will come to recognize and accept that critical thinking will not guarantee that you find an answer to every question or a solution to every problem. Sometimes you will reach the conclusion that you just don't know, and that's okay in its own right. No matter how much our brains crave certainty, sometimes we just have to tolerate a level of uncertainty in our lives. After all, it is impossible to ever know exactly what is in store for us.

A story:

We know uncertainty can be uncomfortable. Sure, we may like to know exactly what lies ahead so we can be prepared. Our brains are even hardwired to want constant certainty. But life doesn't work that way. We must learn to tolerate some level of uncertainty in order to function. How great is your tolerance for uncertainty? Consider the following questions and judge for yourself how well you can tolerate uncertainty.

- Do you often want reassurance and approval from others before you are willing to make a decision? This may be about small things like what style of haircut you should get or outfit you should wear, or big things like relationship advice, major purchases, or career decisions. You may find yourself almost paralyzed to make a decision on your own because you fear an unknown outcome.

- Do you find yourself making lists for everything? If you need a list to keep track of your lists, you might be relying on them for comfort and security when you are facing uncertainty.

- Are you famous for checking and rechecking everything? If so, you may be craving more certainty in your life.

- Do you have a hard time sharing responsibility or delegating tasks to others? If you think things are best handled by you in order to turn out the way you expect, you may have a low level of tolerance for uncertainty and prefer to be in control by doing everything yourself.

- Do you find yourself constantly wanting to stay busy so that you don't have time to think about other things? I was this way when my mom was very sick. I had to keep myself busy because the fear of the unknown was too much for me to take. I wanted to avoid the stress and fear from a sad and uncertain situation at every cost. I threw myself into work and helping to care for her so that my mind never had time to wander to darker places.

- Are you a procrastinator? This may not stem from just wanting to avoid tasks because you don't like them; it may be more deeply rooted in avoiding tasks because you can't be certain that you will be successful.

Did you discover that you are more intolerant to uncertainty than you previously thought? Don't worry—you are not alone. We are all intolerant, to a certain degree. Since we will never be able to completely erase uncertainty from our lives, try as we may, we must strive to raise our level of tolerance for it.

Exercise:

Begin by thinking about the things that cause you anxiety in your life. Rank them in order from the ones that cause you the most significant amounts of worry and stress to the ones that may simply be more minor annoyances. Now flip your list and write them down in order from the one that causes you the least anxiety to the one that causes you the most.

Think of this as your letting things go to-do list. Look at it the first item on your list. Maybe it is wondering if you brought your lunch with you as you are driving on your way to work. Think about the worst-case scenarios that are possible. If you forgot your lunch, you may either have to spend money to buy lunch that day, or if you didn't bring money with you, you may have to skip lunch. In either case, you will survive. While skipping a meal may not be your first choice, you will not starve, and if you are concerned about the consequences that buying lunch may have on your budget or waistline, commit to an extra 15 minutes on the treadmill, or to not buying an espresso another day to make up for it.

In any case, avoid the urge to pull over and check to see if your lunch is in the back seat or to turn around and go home to check. Everything will be okay, no matter what. Once you are comfortable tolerating that level of uncertainty, move on to the second item on your list and address that uncertainty in the same manner. It will take practice and may be uncomfortable, but gradually, you will begin to increase your level of tolerance for uncertainty over time.

If you start with the things in your life that cause you the least anxiety, practice increasing your tolerance of uncertainty associated with them and then work your way up, you will experience greater success and be less likely to give in to fear.

Assess your progress by asking yourself some critical thinking questions:

- Did things turn out okay, even though you were uncertain?
- If not, what happened? Try to look at the situation objectively.
- Were you able to make adjustments and deal with the negative outcome?
    - If you were, how did you handle it?

            - If you weren't, what could you have done differently?
    - How might you be able to deal with negative outcomes that arise in the future?

Sometimes things turn out the way we hope, and sometimes they don't. That's just the nature of life. There will be good and bad events in your life—there's nothing you can do about that. The best thing you can do is increase your level of tolerance for uncertainty, improve your responses when negative outcomes arise, and just live your life to the fullest while being a critical thinker.

Key takeaways:

- Always ask questions. Information is your best friend as you strive to become a more critical thinker.

- Frame your questions neutrally and objectively so that you may find the truth instead of partial or misleading answers.

- Be aware of the biases that exist in yourself and others, and think critically to overcome them.

- Emotional reasoning can be harmful, unless it is balanced with critical thinking.

- Over-generalizations are the enemy of critical thinking. Don't rush to judge the whole group based on the actions and characteristics of a few.

- Avoid the projection bias of assuming that everyone will think the same way you do. Be open to other explanations and interpretations before you reach a conclusion.

- Practice increasing your level of tolerance to uncertainty. It won't be a quick or easy solution. It will take time and effort, but it will make life less stressful and more enjoyable over time.

Chapter 3: Piaget's Theory on Thinking

Jean Piaget is a renowned Swiss psychologist who was a pioneer in studying the cognitive development of children from birth. While his work in this field was published in 1936, it still plays a vital role in the education of children today. Prior to his research, children were largely thought of as mini-adults and many people thought their intelligence was predetermined.

This chapter will discuss how human cognition is developed from birth. Through Piaget's theory of cognitive development, we will see how we acquire more knowledge gradually over time and why it is so important to learn critical thinking skills at an early age.

Piaget believed that children move through four stages as they develop mentally. He considered children active participants in their learning process. He thought they observe and explore as they try to make sense of their world, and that as they interact with things around them, they continue to gain new knowledge as they build on and expand the knowledge they already have.[ix]

How did Piaget develop his theory?

Piaget was born in Switzerland in 1896. Growing up, he was a gifted student who published his first scientific paper at the young age of 11 and always loved learning. He was influenced by the work of Alfred Binet and Theodore De Simon, who he assisted as they tried to standardize the IQ tests they developed for children. It was when Piaget was scoring the children's IQ tests that he began to notice patterns in the questions that younger children consistently got wrong, which were different from the ones older children and adults typically missed. That, along with his observations of his daughter and nephew, inspired his interest in further studying the cognitive development of children and supported his developing hypothesis that children's brains are different from adult brains (not just smaller versions of adult minds, as had previously been thought).

Piaget came to believe that a child's intelligence grows and develops over time as it moves through four stages. He found that there are concrete differences in the brains of younger and older children. It is not simply that older children could think more quickly than their younger counterparts. He reasoned that children are not less intelligent than adults, they just think differently. Piaget's theory of cognitive development has had an enduring impact on the field of education that is present even today as it has helped to shape the instructional strategies and curriculum that have been developed to present information to children in a way that ensures they are developmentally able to receive it.

A look at Piaget's four stages of cognitive development

<u>The Sensorimotor Stage</u>

Birth to two years old

Characteristics of this stage:

- Children discover the world through their senses and movements.
- Looking, listening, and grasping are some of the ways they gather information.
- They learn that objects still exist, even when they can no longer see them (i.e.,

their mother is still around, even though she may walk into another room), which is called object permanence. This is why playing peek-a-boo can be so important at this age.
- Children learn that their actions can make things happen in their world (i.e., if they throw their bottle on the floor, someone will pick it up for them) and they like to test this theory often.
- They learn that objects and people are separate and unique things, and they are able to begin to give them names (i.e., Daddy, ball, bear, etc.).[x]

There is a whole lot of growth and learning going on during this stage! Kids are constantly making new discoveries about themselves and the world around them. It is during the sensorimotor stage that children learn to crawl and walk. Their language development grows by leaps and bounds as they listen to and observe others. Piaget believed the concept of object permanence was one of the most important developments children in this stage make.

A child in this stage may perform an action by accident, such as squealing, sucking their thumb, or putting things in their mouth, and then learn to intentionally repeat it because they like it. This is also why they will intentionally drop an object over and over when they discover that someone will pick it up for them.

Children in the sensorimotor stage learn from imitating what they see and hear others do and from trying new things. For example, they learn that banging on a pot makes a loud sound or pushing a button makes a toy light up, and they enjoy repeating these activities many times. Near the end of this stage, children begin to recognize that pictures and even sign language can represent objects in the world. For instance, they will recognize themselves or family members in pictures, or begin to use signs to indicate that they are hungry or thirsty, since not being able to fully articulate what they want and need is a source of frustration for them.

<u>The Preoperational Stage</u>

From 2-7 years old

Characteristics of this stage:

- Children can use words and pictures to represent objects during this stage.
- The focus of children at this age tends to be on themselves so they have a hard time understanding the feelings of others.
- Language and thinking skills are still greatly improving, but they are not able to think of things that are more abstract. They are concrete thinkers in this stage and have difficulty in making logical connections.[xi]

It is less important to focus intently on the exact ages of each of Piaget's stages than it is to recognize the order in which they occur and the approximate time frames. There will always be children who enter each stage at a younger or older age than Piaget suggests, and there is no need to hold fast to strict expectations of exactly when a child should be in each stage.

The major development in this stage is language development. While this began during the sensorimotor stage, their use of language will really explode during the preoperational stage. Their vocabulary will increase greatly as they really begin to understand the words they use in their speech. They will be much less frustrated as people are able to understand more of what they are trying to say.

Another major milestone during the preoperational stage is an increase in play and their ability to pretend. Children in this stage will likely enjoy pretending that they are a vet, doctor, mom, dad, or other careers and activities that they observe adults participating in. They will enjoy pretending to cook things in a kitchen, or doing other household chores such as mowing the grass, sweeping the floor, or washing the clothing and dishes.

They will likely still have difficulty sharing or understanding the point of view of others during this age, as everything in their minds still belongs to or is all about them. They have a very egocentric view of the world at this stage.

Children in the preoperational stage have problems recognizing objects as having the same size if they are in a different shape or placed in a different-sized container. For example, you may cut a piece of paper in half going from top to bottom or side to side. Even though all of the pieces are exactly half of the same size of a piece of paper, a child in this stage would likely not recognize that they are the same size because they are different shapes. Along the same lines, if you poured a cup of water into a tall, skinny glass and then transferred the same water into a shorter glass, the children would not typically identify the two glasses as having held the same amount of water because the shape of the glasses was different. Even if the children would watch you pouring the water, nearly every time they would identify the glass that looked like it was fuller as holding more water than the other shape of glass.[xii]

The Concrete Operational Stage

From 7 to 11 years old

Characteristics of this stage:

- Children begin to think more logically about concrete things. Their thinking becomes more systematic and organized. Abstract concepts are still largely beyond their understanding at this stage. They still take things very literally.

- They begin to understand that the size of an object can still be the same even if the shape of it or its container is different. For example, the amount of water in a tall, skinny glass can be the same even if it is poured into a short, wide glass.
- Children in the concrete operational stage become less egocentric and can understand the feelings and point of view of others much more easily than they ever could before.[xiii]

Children now take ownership of their feelings and opinions and realize that others do not necessarily think and feel the same way they do. They see themselves as a unique individual during this stage.

If you take two pizzas that are the same size and cut one into four equal-sized pieces, and cut the other one into eight equal-sized pieces, children in this stage will be able understand that each pizza is still the same amount of food. This is a marked difference from the earlier stages.

Children at this stage are now able to remember the steps of a process in any order without having to rely on adults for consistent prompting. They are also able to focus on more than one part of a problem at a time. This is certainly helpful as the academic challenges these children face begin to get more complex and involve more steps. Students in the concrete operational stage are better able to follow multi-step directions.

The Formal Operational Stage

From 12 years old and up to adulthood

Characteristics of this stage:

- Children in the formal operational stage are now able to think more abstractly and hypothetically.
- They start to think about more abstract concepts such as moral, ethical, philosophical, social, and

political issues in the world and form their own thoughts and opinions about them.
- They can now use logic and reasoning to move from something general down to something more specific.
- Children in this stage can now see more than one possible solution to a problem and can begin to take a more scientific approach to analyzing and solving problems.[xiv]

The ability to think about abstract concepts in a logical way is a major shift in this stage. Piaget did not believe that children only gain new knowledge as they get older; he also believed that there are fundamental changes in the ways children in the different cognitive stages see their world. The shift to abstract thinking is one of those changes. Every stage has them.

The thinking of children in the formal operational stage becomes much more complex and advanced than it has been in the previous stages. Children do not have to rely solely on their past experiences to shape their understanding of the world.

Now they are able to imagine possible outcomes and consequences that may arise from their actions, or the actions of others well beyond whatever they have previously experienced in their own lives.

Children in this stage are able to comprehend and offer possible solutions and outcomes from if-then scenarios that they must imagine and be able to interpret. The level of their critical thinking and cognition is at its deepest during the formal operational stage. Some people may never fully reach this stage of cognitive development, while others may only briefly enter it (perhaps during a challenging class) without being able to maintain the level of effort that this higher thinking requires for the long-term.

Piaget was keenly aware that there are other factors that influence the growth and intellectual development of children. Some of them are:

Schemas

According to Piaget, a schema is a category of knowledge into which (children's) brains place the new information that they learn, and it is also the process they go through to get new knowledge. Schemas are a way to organize information so the learning may be readily retrieved when the child needs it. As children experience new things, they gather new information about the world and their brains take it in. That new information either adds to or changes the schemas that are already in place in their brains.

For example, a child may have a schema about men. Perhaps early in life every man they have known was someone's dad. Since the child's only life experience was with men who were fathers, the child might believe that all men are dads. As the child encounters more and more men in their life, they are sure to come across some men who do not have children. The child will take in that new knowledge and use it to change the schema they previously held so that it will include the new information they learned. Their definition of a man will expand to include men who are fathers as well as men who are not.[xv]

Assimilation

Piaget refers to the act of bringing in new information to schemas that are already present in the brain as assimilation. If we stick with the example of the child learning about men, every time a child sees a man and identifies him as such, the child is assimilating the male into the schema they already have about men. The human brain has a tendency to tweak or alter the information we learn a bit in order to make it fit more easily with the ideas and theories we already have. We should be aware of this shortcut the brain automatically takes as we maintain our focus on critical thinking.

Accommodation

According to Piaget, accommodation occurs when children learn new information that doesn't fit exactly in the schemas that are already in their brain as-is. Accommodation involves altering the schemas that were already there as they gather new information that results in the need to adjust their previously held learning. New schemas can also be created during accommodation. In our example above, when the child learned that a male doesn't have to have children in order to be a man, they demonstrated accommodation when they took that new information and used it to alter their previous definition of a man to include both males who do and do not have children.[xvi]

Equilibration

Piaget called the desire that all children have to find a balance between accommodation and assimilation equilibration. Equilibration enables children to advance to the next stage of cognitive development once they have found the balance between simply applying the new knowledge they gather (assimilation) and having to alter their previously held beliefs as they gather new information that disproves or expands those beliefs (accommodation). If that balance is not achieved, they are not ready to move on to the next, more challenging level of cognitive development. If children have to constantly change every belief they have, it would be mentally exhausting. They would need to spend more time growing, practicing, and developing in their current stage before they would be developmentally ready to advance to the next level.[xvii]

Piaget increased the level of insight and understanding people had for how children develop mentally when he shared his theory of cognitive development with the world. It proved that children are actually active participants in their learning process. They do not just sit back and wait for others to give them information. They are always exploring the world around them and using their learning to increase their understanding of how things work.

Piaget's theory has stood the test of time and had an undeniably major impact on the way our children are taught even today, but there is currently another movement in education that is also guiding the way schools instruct our youth. It is the push for schools to stress the importance of teaching critical thinking skills to students from a young age.

Educators and the business community alike support this movement as the goal is to create students who are strong critical thinkers are ready to use those skills across all academic subject matters and in all areas of their lives. When trying to adequately prepare students for life and learning in the 21st century and beyond, critical thinking is a crucial component if we hope to have well-educated young adults who are career-minded, driven, and ready to accept the responsibilities that go along with being good global citizens. The focus on critical thinking strives to ensure students are fully prepared and equipped with the skills necessary to be successful in all forms of higher education and the modern workplaces of today and tomorrow. Our world continues to become more complex and competitive by the minute, and our youth need strong critical thinking skills in order to face the challenges that life will throw at them.

Critical thinking is such a vital skill to have in the 21st century that an entire educational movement was formed around it. It is so important to begin building the critical thinking skills in our children as soon as possible so they can become second nature to them. But it is never too late for anyone willing to put forth the time and effort to hone and improve their critical thinking skills.

Key takeaways:

- Before the work of Jean Piaget, it was largely assumed that children's brains were just smaller versions of adult brains and their capacity for intellectual development was largely predetermined.
- After Piaget presented his theory of cognitive development, people came to understand that children are active participants in their own learning and they are not less intelligent than adults; their brains simply learn in a different way.
- Piaget's theory had a profound and lasting impact on the way that children are taught in our schools. His four stages of

cognitive development are largely responsible for establishing the curriculum our children are presented with and the instructional strategies they are taught to use.
- In the quest for success for our youth in the 21st century, there is an educational movement that stresses the need for teaching critical thinking skills to our children from an early age in order to give them the greatest opportunity for success in an increasingly complex and competitive world.

Chapter 4: The Science of Paul-Elder

Why is critical thinking challenging?

Everyone thinks—our brains are hardwired to do so. But if we sit back and leave our brains to their own devices, chances are the thoughts they produce will most likely be biased, uniformed, partial, incorrect, or even stereotypical and judgmental of others. Since the quality of our lives is directly connected to the quality of our thoughts, opinions, and ideas, we should never be content to leave our thinking to chance. If we do not produce strong quality thoughts, we will not be able to live our lives to the fullest and achieve our true potential. However, these quality thoughts do not come easily or occur automatically. A commitment to put forth effort and really practice the art of critical thinking is imperative to our success.[xviii]

What exactly is critical thinking?

Critical thinking is the art of always asking questions and examining our thinking with the goal of constantly improving it. Strong critical thinkers are able to objectively gather information so that informed and quality conclusions can be made.

How do you know if you are a critical thinker?

People with excellent critical thinking skills:

- are able to generate quality questions and identify problems accurately and plainly;
- can readily and objectively gather, evaluate, and interpret new information;
- take the time and put forth the effort to be sure any conclusions they reach or possible solutions they come up with are of the highest quality and are well-thought-out;
- are open-minded to the perspectives of others and are willing to consider thoughts and opinions that differ from their own;

- recognize the biases and baggage they bring with them and work hard to address and overcome them;
- can positively and effectively communicate their thoughts and ideas to others as they try to work together to come up with solutions and explanations to difficult problems.[xix]

In order to be a strong critical thinker, people must be able to monitor their own thinking in order to make the necessary changes once they receive information which refutes their previously held beliefs. They should be mindful of their personal cognitive biases and be prepared to take action to overcome them. They must demonstrate a willingness to practice and continue to develop and improve their critical thinking skills. They should be empathetic and humble, knowing that the opinions and perspectives of others are to be valued and may offer great insights to identifying problems and possible solutions because they themselves do not have all the answers.

The essential dimensions of critical thinking

Dr. Richard Paul, the Director of Research and Professional Development at the Center for Critical Thinking and former Chair of the National Council for Excellence in Critical Thinking, wrote numerous books and articles on the subject that garnered him world renown. He worked with his wife, Dr. Linda Elder, an educational psychologist, author, teacher, and presenter who is also recognized as an authority on critical thinking. She is the President of the Foundation for Critical Thinking as well as the Executive Director of the Center for Critical Thinking. Together, along with other colleagues, Paul and Elder identified the following essential dimensions of critical thinking:

The universal intellectual standards[xx]

Universal intellectual standards are standards which have to be utilized anytime you are trying to critically analyze your thinking about a problem or theory. It is impossible to truly think critically without a great understanding and mastery of these standards. You may need to be prompted with these questions as you practice holding yourself accountable for your thinking at first, but over time, this line of self-questioning should become automatic. We know our brains try to take the easy path and rely on biases to make new information fit with the beliefs we already hold. If we want to be truly critical thinkers and make informed decisions based on facts, we need to be willing to challenge our own thoughts, rather than passively leaving our brains to work unchecked.

- Clarity: When you seek clarity, you might ask:
    - Can you explain in more detail?
    - Can you provide examples?

If information we are gathering is unclear, we won't be able to assess its accuracy, objectivity, or relevance. Defining a problem more clearly may be necessary before true analysis and critical thinking can begin.

- Accuracy: When you are trying to determine the accuracy of information, you might ask:
    - How could we verify that?
    - Do any other sources support those findings?

- Precision: When you are trying to increase precision, you may ask:
    - Can you be more specific?
    - Can you be more detailed in your description?

- Relevance: When you are trying to determine the relevance of a piece of information, you may ask:
    - How is that connected to the problem at hand?
    - How does it help us solve the problem?

- Depth: When you are trying to determine the depth of information, you might ask:
    - What makes this challenging?
    - What are some difficulties we are going to have to overcome?

- Breadth: When addressing the breadth of information, you may need to consider:
    - Do we need to consider any other points of view?
    - Are there any other ways we can look at this?

- Logic: When you need to see if the information is logical, you may ask:
    - Does this information make sense with the other information we have?
    - Does this go along with the evidence and fit into the bigger picture?

- Significance: When considering the significance of information, you might ask:
    - Is this the most important thing we should think about?
    - Which is the most important idea for us to address?

- Fairness: To ensure fairness, you want to consider:
    - Have all perspectives been heard and represented?
    - Are any of the facts being altered to support a certain opinion over others?
    - Are all points of view being given equal deference?

The elements of thinking:

Dr. Richard Paul and Dr. Linda Elder also identified eight elements of thinking that they believed people needed to master in order to improve their thinking:

1. **Purpose**
   All thinking has a purpose behind it which must be considered. The purpose is the goal you are trying to achieve. The purpose must be clear. It might be to solve a problem, answer a question, or increase understanding, but you must know where you are going or you will never know when you get there. Be sure to check in with your purpose frequently to make sure you are still on target with what you'd like to accomplish, and that you haven't veered off track.

2. **Question**
   The question will guide your thinking and must be very clear and precise. It will be the driving force as you seek information and it must be worded carefully, or it may allow you to get off track and not get the information you desire. You can break the overarching question down into smaller, more manageable underlying questions, if

it helps to maintain your focus and direction.

3. **Assumptions**

   Assumptions are the beliefs you hold that you don't give much thought to. They may even be kept in your subconscious. Recognize how your assumptions have a major impact on the way you view the world. You should periodically assess your beliefs to make sure they are supported by evidence.

4. **Point of View**

   It is important to never assume that your point of view is the only one or that it is more important than others. The way that you see the world is only one lens through which it can be viewed. All viewpoints must be considered and given equal weight and deference when analyzing your thinking. Be fair when analyzing opinions that are different from yours.

5. **Information**

   The information that you try to gather to answer a question or solve a problem needs to be accurate, relevant, and backed up by facts and evidence. You will need to make sure that your personal cognitive biases and opinions don't distort the way you evaluate information. Objectivity and open-mindedness are crucial. Be willing to gather evidence that both supports and disputes your ideas for analysis.

6. **Inferences**

   Inferences are the conclusions your mind reaches as it tries to make sense of the information it is presented with. Your inferences need to be based on the facts of the evidence you find. They should make logical sense and be consistent with each other.

7. **Concepts**

   Concepts are the ideas and theories you generate as you try to make sense of what is going on in the world around you. You need to understand the ideas and theories you give prominence in your life and make sure that you have justification for them. Be certain that you have explored alternative explanations and that you can explain your ideas and concepts clearly.

8. **Implications and Consequences**

   Implications arise from your thoughts. Critical thinkers consider the implications of their thoughts before they plan a course of action. Consequences arise from your actions. You should always think through what might happen if you make a decision to act and what could happen if you decide not to act. Consider all possible implications and consequences and recognize that not all of them will be positive.[xxi]

Valuable Intellectual Traits

Another component of the Paul and Elder critical thinking system are the valuable intellectual traits. These are the traits that Paul and Elder deemed necessary for people to have in order to become strong critical thinkers:

Intellectual Humility

Intellectual humility is admitting that you are human and there are limits to the knowledge you have. It involves recognizing you possess cognitive and personal biases, and that your brain tends to see things in such a way that your opinions and viewpoints are favored above others. It is being willing to work to overcome those biases in order to be more objective and make informed decisions. People who display intellectual humility are more likely to be receptive to learning from others who think differently than they do. They tend to be well-liked and respected by others because they make it clear that they value what other people bring to the table. Intellectually humble people want to learn more and are open to finding information from a variety of sources. They are not interested in trying to appear or feel superior to others.

When I think of an intellectually humble person, my dad comes to my mind. He played sports in high school and was offered a college scholarship to play football. He was eager to accept it, but his parents needed his help at home on the family farm. He decided to decline the scholarship and not attend college. He went on to continue farming and also worked as a school bus driver and high school basketball referee in order to financially support our family.

Missing out on a college education always bothered my dad. He was determined that all of his kids would be able to attend college no matter what. He became our biggest supporter and cheerleader as we worked hard to earn good grades. When we attended college, he was always eager to live and learn vicariously through us and our experiences. He wanted us to talk to him about what we learned in our classes and the fun we were having at school. He was happy to sit and listen for hours to our stories. He understood clearly that there were limits to his own knowledge and was eager to learn from his children.[xxii]

Intellectual Courage

Intellectual courage is not refusing to back away from beliefs and viewpoints you have strong negative feelings about, but rather, it's about being willing to face them and listen with an open mind before passing judgement on them. You need to be willing to accept quality evidence, even if it disagrees with your own views, and be ready to use it to modify your thinking, if warranted. It is important to look at information through a critical thinking lens and really evaluate it—not just accept ideas that are popular with others. People who demonstrate intellectual courage are willing to take risks if it means they will learn the truth in the end.

I recently read of a mother named Rukiye. Her son, Suliman Ahmed Abdulmutakallim, was serving in the U.S. Navy in Iraq, where he was shot by three young men, one of whom was 14. They stole his money and the food he was taking home for him and his wife and left him lying in the street to die. When Rukiye faced one of his killers in court, she hugged him and his mother and told them she forgave him. She believed her son's death was ordained and that she needed to make something good come of it, because perhaps the reason for his death was to save and turn around the life of his killer. She said she wanted to listen to him and become part of his life so she could learn how to help him so that he never takes another life. I can't even imagine the strength that took. I think Rukiye is the epitome of an example of intellectual courage.[xxiii]

Intellectual Empathy

Intellectual empathy is putting yourself in another's shoes to try to understand their thoughts and perspective. It involves overcoming our tendency to give more weight to our own viewpoint and trying to see things through another's eyes. People who are intellectually empathetic are willing to accept that there are people who have viewpoints which differ from their own, and they are no less important. Intellectual empathy means that you may have to accept that you are wrong at times, even when you are convinced you are right. In trying to be intellectually empathetic, you need to try to look at things from another person's perspective without distorting their thoughts to make them closer to your own.

Intellectual empathy brings to mind a story from my childhood, *The True Story of the Three Little Pigs*. This book told the traditional story of the *Three Little Pigs*, but from the perspective of the big bad wolf. He explained that he was really trying to borrow a cup of sugar so he could make a cake for his grandma, but he had a bad cold and the pigs misunderstood his intentions. By the end of the book, the reader could not help but realize that there are at least two sides to every story, and maybe the big bad wolf wasn't quite so terrible after all. [xxiv]

Intellectual Autonomy

Intellectual autonomy is taking ownership of and accepting responsibility for your own thinking. It involves a commitment to think critically about your thinking. It is holding yourself accountable for analyzing your beliefs to make sure they are based on facts and evidence. People who are intellectually autonomous do not just passively accept the beliefs of others, but rather, are out taking control of their own thinking and making judgments for themselves. They do not give in to social pressure and do not just go along with the crowd. They realize that even experts are human and make mistakes from time to time, so they evaluate all information with a healthy dose of skepticism and critical thinking.[xxv]

During my teaching career, I often found myself exercising intellectual autonomy and refusing to go along blindly with my colleagues or administrators if I feel their proposals are not in our students' best interests. Back then, I considered some of my most important responsibilities to act as an advocate for and as a role model to my students. I took those responsibilities very seriously and always tried to lead by example.

One example was when I stood up to the crowd to exercise intellectual autonomy was when all the students in our school were required to take a very lengthy reading and math exam. The students filled in their answers on bubble sheets (Scantrons) that were fed through a scanner and scored by a computer. The company that created the test inadvertently provided our school with the wrong answer sheets to score the tests against, resulting in the students receiving much lower scores because the computer marked them as missing questions they had really gotten correct.

When the scores were much lower than expected for the entire school, the principals reached out to the testing company for help. It was then they realized they had given our school the wrong answer sheets. All of the teachers rescored their students' tests by hand so that they could see how their students had truly performed on the tests. I was satisfied with that. I had the information I needed about my students so that I could help them to improve their skills, and as far as I was concerned, the process was done.

My principals had another idea in mind, though. They did not like that the incorrect lower scores were sent to the superintendent, and they thought it made the school look bad. Instead of simply explaining the situation and sharing the correct scores with the superintendent, they wanted the entire student body to retake the tests.

I was very upset. I knew how my students would react if they were told they had to completely retake a test when they had done their best and had done nothing wrong. We had mandated state tests coming up in the next few weeks that our kids were going to have to take, and I didn't think it was right to put our students through yet another test just to make our school "look good" to others.

All of my colleagues went along with the principals' request and made their students retake the test. I went to my principals and explained my concerns to them. They ultimately decided to excuse my students from retaking the test. After weighing all of the information, I decided to speak up on behalf of my students and go against the crowd. I thought for myself and made a decision to express my concerns to my administrators instead of just blindly following along with what was expected. That is how intellectual autonomy works.

Intellectual Integrity

Perhaps William Shakespeare best described intellectual integrity when he said, "This above all: to thine own self be true." Intellectual integrity is when you are true to your own thinking and consistently apply the same critical thinking skills to all of the information you analyze. If you display intellectual integrity, you hold everyone—friend, foe, stranger, and yourself—to the same standards of requiring proof and evidence to support their thoughts and opinions. People who practice intellectual integrity practice what they preach to others and lead by example. They know actions speak louder than words, and they live in such a way that they can be proud of the things they do because they are accurate representations of themselves and their character. These people are honest and own it when they make mistakes that need to be corrected.[xxvi]

An example of intellectual integrity occurred in my life when I taught under a principal who had a unique style of leading. He was very outspoken and a little rough around the edges, but he cared about his students and staff, which is something I will always respect. He was not very popular with most of my colleagues because he did not behave in the way principals traditionally did. He had an open door policy, though, and encouraged any staff member who had questions and concerns to go to his office and speak to him about them because he was always willing to listen.

It was during this particular school year that some of my close teacher friends and I decided we could no longer eat in the teacher's lounge because we felt like hypocrites. It had become such a negative place where it seemed that all anyone did was complain about students, colleagues, parents, or administrators. We decided we did not want to be a part of all of the negativity, so our group began eating lunch in my classroom every day while our students were at lunch and recess. Some of my colleagues decided to try to get rid of our principal by going behind his back and complaining about the things he did to the superintendent, instead of talking to him about their concerns and giving him a chance to address them.

One day, our principal came down to talk to me in my classroom to ask me if I knew who had it in for him and was trying to get him fired. I felt terrible for him and explained that I can't stand it when people go behind others' backs instead of personally speaking to them and trying to solve problems together like responsible, caring human beings. I told him that I would help him if I could, but I honestly did not know who it was because I had removed myself from the daily negativity of the teacher's lounge, since that was not the type of teacher, or person, I wanted to be.

It kept bothering me the way some people were treating our principals, so I felt like I had to speak up. I returned to the teacher's lounge the next day at lunch and spoke to my colleagues from the heart. I explained that as a human being, I always try to treat people the way I would want to be treated, and as a teacher, I refuse to behave in a way I wouldn't accept from the students in my classroom. I told my colleagues that if they had the same life philosophy I did, to please join me in wanting to be a part of the solution to all the problems and concerns that were so often discussed in the teacher's lounge, and to be willing to work with our entire staff, including our principal, to create the best possible school year for our students.

It was pretty quiet in the room when I left. I know I didn't reach everyone that day, but I did reach some of them. Our principal created an advisory council that met with him twice a month to address concerns of the staff. More people volunteered to be a part of the committee than I expected. Sadly, at the end of the school year, they transferred our principal to another school, but at least his job had been saved, and hopefully some of our characters had been saved that school year too.

Intellectual Perseverance

People who display the trait of intellectual perseverance simply don't give up. Come what may, they have bought in to what it means to be a critical thinker, and they won't be swayed from that. They are committed for the long haul. They understand that things will not always be easy, but they are willing to stick with it and see it through despite frustrations, setbacks, obstacles, difficulties, and challenges from those who oppose their views and are unwilling to even hear them because they know it will all be worth it when they reach the answers and greater understanding they seek.[xxvii]

On February 14, 2018, there was a mass shooting at Marjory Stoneman Douglas High School in Parkland, Florida. Sadly, it is one of the deadliest school shootings in history; 17 students and staff were killed and 17 more were injured. I think the surviving students who have decided to speak up about their feelings after the shooting are an excellent example of what intellectual perseverance is all about, and they are only in high school.

I am not going to speak about whether I think their beliefs are right or wrong. I will not weigh in on the debate over gun control in the United States. That is a mess that is thankfully well above my paygrade. But what I will say is these young ladies and gentlemen have survived tragedy and obstacles that no one ever should have to— especially not at such a young age.

They have gathered information from their own experiences and other places and analyzed it to form their opinions. They are willing to speak publicly about them, despite many Americans being very vocal in their disagreement with those opinions. It is one thing to express anger and disapproval toward a viewpoint, but it is quite another when that anger is directed in personal attacks and threats to people. Regardless of anyone's opinion on any issue, that should never be acceptable. I don't know many adults who would have the intellectual perseverance and fortitude to continue to speak publicly in the face of that, but these high school students are committed to their cause and they continue to stand by their beliefs. That is something I can respect in anyone—whether I agree with them or not.

Confidence in Reason
==

Confidence in reason is a sincere belief that in the long run, truth and reason will prevail. It involves believing that people should be able to draw their own conclusions by moving through their own thought processes. It is trusting that people can become strong, reasonable, rational, critical thinkers over time, and that they will ultimately reach conclusions that are good for humanity.[xxviii]

The first example of confidence in reason that came to my mind is our belief in the United States that having trials where a jury hears and analyzes the evidence in a court case is one of the fairest ways to determine a person's innocence or guilt. We trust jurors to critically analyze the evidence presented by lawyers and witnesses during a trial, and then to objectively reach an agreement, discussing the facts and theories, and even possibly persuading each other to modify their thinking as part of the process. We think that if they are given guidelines regarding the law and guidance and support from the judge, they will be able to uncover the truth and reach a reasonable and rational decision. We trust them to do what is right and reach the correct conclusion about the defendant's guilt or innocence.

Fair-mindedness

Fair-mindedness involves giving all viewpoints the same respect and deference as you listen to them and analyze their arguments. Being fair-minded means considering the perspectives of others and affording them the same value and weight as you do your own even when they are in clear opposition to your beliefs. People who are fair-minded treat every viewpoint in an unbiased and unprejudiced way.[xxix]

There is, sadly, a lot of prejudice in the world today. When I think of the virtue of fair-mindedness, a single image of that went viral on social media comes to my mind. It is an image of two children—one black and one white—who are holding hands. Children are not born with prejudice and hatred toward others in their hearts. They are not born thinking they are better than others. What a wonderful world it would be if children could keep their wide-eyed innocent view of the world and others in that regard, instead of taking on the biased views of the adults in their lives. I would love to see everyone trying to be a little more fair-minded in their daily lives. That would make quite a powerful difference in the world.

Key Takeaways:

- Critical thinking is the art of always asking questions and examining our thinking with the goal of constantly improving it. Strong critical thinkers are committed to objectively gathering information so that they can uncover the truth they seek and make informed, quality conclusions in their lives.
- Dr. Richard Paul and Dr. Linda Elder worked together to identify universal intellectual standards which should be utilized anytime you are trying to critically analyze your thinking about a problem or theory. They include: clarity, accuracy, precision, relevance, depth, breadth, logic, significance, and fairness.
- They went further to identify eight elements of thinking they believed people need to master in order to improve their thinking: purpose, question, assumptions,

point of view, information, inferences, concepts, and implications and consequences.
- Paul and Elder defined a set of valuable intellectual traits they feel all strong critical thinkers should display: humility, courage, empathy, autonomy, integrity, perseverance, confidence in reason, and fair-mindedness.
- To visually summarize the topic of this chapter, here is a great picture:

Critical Thinkers Routinely Apply Intellectual Standards To The Elements Of Reasoning In Order To Develop Intellectual Traits

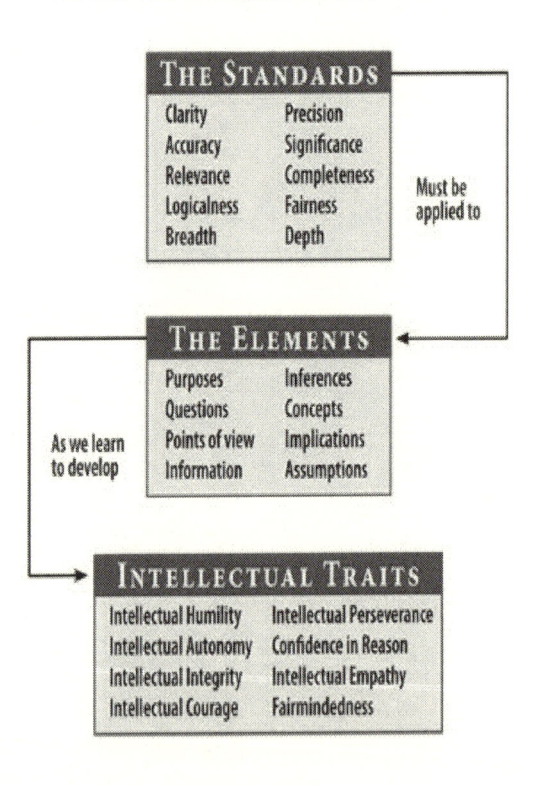

THE STANDARDS

Clarity	Precision
Accuracy	Significance
Relevance	Completeness
Logicalness	Fairness
Breadth	Depth

Must be applied to

THE ELEMENTS

Purposes	Inferences
Questions	Concepts
Points of view	Implications
Information	Assumptions

As we learn to develop

INTELLECTUAL TRAITS

Intellectual Humility	Intellectual Perseverance
Intellectual Autonomy	Confidence in Reason
Intellectual Integrity	Intellectual Empathy
Intellectual Courage	Fairmindedness

Picture I: *The Standards, the elements, and the intellectual traits.*[xxx]

Chapter 5: Understand Deeply

I am in awe of Olympians. Their dedication to their sport is inspiring. Every day, they are willing to do what others won't in order to achieve at the very highest levels. McKayla Maroney is one of those Olympians. She rose to the pinnacle of her sport as a gold-medal-winning member of the United States Women's Gymnastics Team at the 2012 Summer Olympics in London, where she also won an individual silver medal in the vault. She is younger than I am, but I think she showed she is wise beyond her years when she said, "Don't practice till you get it right, practice till you can't get it wrong."

This gives us a glimpse into what this chapter is all about. While most people are content with knowing just a little about a lot of things, that simply isn't good enough for a strong critical thinker. They are not satisfied with having such a shallow and simplistic view of the world. Critical thinkers understand the knowledge imparted by actress Helen Hayes when she said, "An expert at anything was once a beginner." They realize that if they want to have mastery over complex information, they must first gain a deeper understanding and mastery over simple things. Critical thinkers are always striving to increase the breadth and depth of their base of knowledge. They make a conscious choice to persevere in their quest for a deeper understanding, when they could easily do what the majority of other people do: give up as soon as something becomes difficult or loses their attention.

This chapter is largely inspired by the work of Edward B. Burger and Michael Starbird from their book *The Five Elements of Effective Thinking*. I think you will find their insights to be helpful as you try to understand the things in your life more deeply.

A story:

I live in a "touristy" part of the United States. I love my home for many reasons and very few of them are how the tourists choose to spend their time. I get friends and family visiting constantly throughout the year, especially during the colder months, and I am in awe of how much they continue to engage in the typical tourist activities even after several years of coming to visit. Part of me is saddened that all of the visitors to our area are so engrossed in our well-advertised tourist industry that they miss out on what really makes it so special. But the other part of me is more selfish and thinks perhaps it is for the best, because if the tourists do see what makes us special, our population might grow exponentially.

I think it is my personal experience that influences the way I choose to spend my vacations. One vacation I have enjoyed over the past few years is taking the occasional cruise. When my family has had a particularly busy or stressful time and we are in need of just a few days to rest and decompress, we sometimes will book a quick last-minute cruise.

In my mind, the biggest bonus to taking a cruise is how little effort and planning it requires. Room and board, transportation, and entertainment is all taken care of, which makes the whole excursion stress-free. While I like that aspect of a cruise for a quick getaway, it made me feel a little hypocritical because I realize it is quite tourist-like. One thing I didn't want was for us to make stops in other countries without my kids getting to know at least a little something about them. I didn't want them to stick to just the shops at the shore where the cruise ship docks or the "ship to shore" excursions that the cruise line schedules. Those only offer the shallowest views imaginable of the countries. That's not what I want for my kids or myself. I want us to have a deeper understanding of everywhere we visit whether it is a city in the United States or a country abroad. I want us to get a feel for the country through the eyes of the people who live there.

So while I enjoy cocktails by the pool, or the seemingly unlimited food at the buffet, I do a bit of online research on the history of the countries where we will dock and the local places that those who live there frequent. I do my best to make arrangements that, although very limited in time, give us a sense of what makes the country special. At least when we board the cruise ship again, it is with a little deeper understanding of the country's identity than we had before. Once in a while, we even decide to return on a longer vacation so we can experience even more of the country's unique flavor.

Understand the fundamentals and go for depth

Burger and Starbird believe that "Any subject or concept (no matter how complex they are) is just a combination of a few simple core ideas. The fundamentals always govern concepts all around us."

Think of anything that you have learned. Whether it was learning your sight words and multiplication facts or how to ride a bike as a child, it likely opened up a whole new world to you, because suddenly reading and math weren't so difficult and didn't take you so long to work through, and riding a bike made you feel all grown up and gave you a feeling of freedom you'd never had before. All of those new, basic skills laid the foundation for you to be able to do more and more wonderful and challenging things as you continued to learn and grow.

Once you have mastered the basics and have a strong foundation, you will find yourself returning to lean on them as you are presented with more difficult things. No matter the skill—whether learning to drive or cook, or studying quantum physics—this will be true. The basic skills you learned will forever be with you and will be so helpful as you continue to build on them adding more complex skills along the way.

We all carry baggage with us wherever we go. Our biases and preconceived ideas are very much a part of us. We hold dear values and beliefs which aren't always based on facts and evidence. If we are going to truly come to a deeper understanding of things in life, we will have to recognize our own baggage and constantly work to overcome it. It is only then that we will be open-minded enough to truly receive new ideas.

The path to deeper understanding begins with a firm grasp of basic ideas and skills. It is impossible to achieve the depth we want and get through the complex without first getting a handle on the basics.

When you are presented with a complex concept, think of it like a swimming pool. If you try to just jump right in the deep end, you might find that you are in over your head. But if you enter in the familiar shallow end, you can work your way to the deep end at your own pace. In other words, take a complex concept and break it down into simpler, more manageable parts. Work on the simpler concepts and then move ahead to the more complex in order to gain a deeper understanding.

First, figure out what's really important. Get to the heart of the matter and clear out the extras that you don't need at first. Master the basics and don't allow the rest to overwhelm you. After you have understood the basics, then you can bring the other stuff back in. It's a lot like when I attempt to assemble my kids' toys. I have learned from experience to just lay out the pieces and sort them into groups first. Then I look at the big picture of the finished product. Sometimes I will even look at online reviews for advice from parents who have already assembled them, and jot that advice down on a piece of paper so I can refer to it when it will come in handy. What I absolutely refuse to do is look through the whole set of instructions at the beginning because it would probably make my head hurt. Just knowing there are 87 steps would completely overwhelm me and make me think I'm in way over my head. So I just take it one step at a time and work on the basic foundation. Once I have that mastered, I congratulate myself on being a skilled engineer and move on to the next step.

This doesn't mean that you will always ignore the extras. That wouldn't lead you to a deeper understanding at all. The point is to just concentrate on the core fundamentals and get back to the basics first when you are just learning something new. Then when you are ready to receive the information, add in the depth.

There are many advantages to breaking down a complex concept into smaller, more manageable parts. Some of them include:

- you can give your attention to the heart of the problem right away
- it allows you to more readily see how the parts are connected to each other
- when you have mastered the basics, you can be more creative
- you are more productive because you are getting something accomplished from the very beginning
- you can see yourself making progress so you feel less stressed and more confident

Make mistakes and raise questions

Many people fear making mistakes because they think it reflects badly upon them, but mistakes are really just learning opportunities in disguise. A mistake is a chance to try harder—not something to cover up and be ashamed of. When we make mistakes, we can learn from them if we take the time to analyze what went wrong. We can find out where our understanding is lacking and fill in the gaps. Mistakes are simply feedbacks that help us to continue to improve. They show us not only what we are doing wrong, but also what we are doing right. They should give us some direction as we keep trying to figure out a solution to the problem.

It is hard to know if our ideas will work without actually testing them. Try as we might to envision every possible outcome and consequence of our ideas, we will always miss some unless we put them into action. We can't let our fear of failing prevent us from learning and making progress.

Michael Jordan is a great example of someone who understood this well. He was cut from his high school basketball team. He easily could have looked at that as defeat and given up, thinking that he was a failure, but he didn't. He chose to learn from the experience and work even harder to improve his skills. He went on to win six championships and five MVPs in his career, and is arguably considered the greatest basketball player of all time. Michael Jordan expressed his feelings on making mistakes when he said, "I have missed more than 9,000 shots in my career. I have lost almost 300 games. On 26 occasions, I have been entrusted to take the game-winning shot, and I missed. I have failed over and over and over again in my life. And that is why I succeed."[xxxi]

Being willing to make mistakes is only one important ingredient in achieving deeper understanding.

Raising questions is another.

It has been said that "if you only do what you've always done, then you will always get what you always got." While there is some debate on who to attribute the quote to, the wisdom in the words definitely applies to our quest for greater understanding.

Often, people assume that just because something has been done with some success in the past, it shouldn't be questioned. Nothing could be further from the truth. We are all works in progress, and so are our ideas and theories. There is always room for growth and improvement. We should never assume that one idea or solution is definitively the best way of doing things. Everything is worth examining critically to see if any improvements can be made.

Burger and Starbird believe asking questions is a key element to effective learning and that assumptions should be challenged, whether they are our own or belong to others. It is all a part of the learning process. Asking questions doesn't reflect badly upon the person who asks them. It simply shows their willingness to learn new things.

In *The Five Elements of Effective Thinking*, Burger and Starbird stress the importance of asking questions as a way to better learn from our mistakes. Besides the obvious questions of

- What went wrong?
- What can I learn from my mistakes?
- What can I do differently in the future?[xxxii]

that we ask when we make our own mistakes, they also believe that it is equally possible, and perhaps more beneficial, to learn from the mistakes of others as well. They think there is much to be learned from the successes and failures of others.

In order to find out what you are doing that *is* working well, be sure to analyze your successes too. You might ask:

- Why did this work?
- How can it be repeated again in the future?
- What went right?

Burger and Starbird talk about one of the greatest philosophers in the world, Socrates. They recognize his great skill in raising questions.

Socrates never thought of himself as having great wisdom—he just knew he sought it all throughout his life. Socrates famously said, "One thing only I know, and that is that I know nothing." He was always asking questions and he asked far more than he answered. His Socratic Method stressed the importance of asking questions about everything.

When we ask questions, we are thinking critically. And it is through our critical thinking that we are able to gain a deeper understanding of ourselves and the world around us. It is important not only to question new ideas and information that we learn, but also the beliefs and convictions that we hold near and dear to our hearts. It is good to frequently evaluate them to be certain they are based on facts and evidence.

Follow the flow of ideas and embrace change

There is always more to be learned. Be a detective and follow the flow of ideas, wherever it may lead, in order to get to the truth. It is entirely possible and even quite likely that you will come to make new discoveries. Build on what others have already learned. Question and confirm their findings and then expand them to make new discoveries of your own.

One thing is certain about life—it is constantly changing. I always knew that as a teacher I was trying to prepare my students for jobs in the future which might not even exist today. I was cognizant every day that the best thing I could do for my students would be to instill in them a love of learning. That would encourage them to never stop questioning and to be lifelong learners. Then come what may in the future, as long as I had taught them strong critical thinking and research skills, they would be able to learn the skills they would need for any career. While I was aware that what I would teach them other skills that would probably become obsolete, the ability to think critically and challenge theories, adjusting or changing their own beliefs and ideas when necessary, never would.

Burger and Starbird reasoned that "Everything great that has ever happened to humanity has begun with an idea in someone's mind. So in order to create something, you need a constant flow of ideas. Everything, whether it's a physical product, a concept, or an idea came from someplace, it has arrived where it is now and is going to change in the future. It's a constant evolution."[xxxiii]

A new idea is not the end, it is simply a beginning—a block, if you will, that can be built upon by countless others and taken in directions we may have never imagined in order to lead us to new and important discoveries. Much like a pebble tossed in the water, the ripples from a new idea extend in all directions, and where its influence stops, no one can be sure.

Thomas Edison summed this idea up nicely when he wrote, "I start where the last man left off." He also went on to say, "Many of life's failures are people who didn't realize how close they were to success when they gave up."

Knowledge is power. We do the best we can with what we have and then when we know better, we do better. As we think critically, we gain better information. When we have better information, we can make more informed, better decisions. Taking in information from a variety of sources and analyzing it leads to deeper understanding. Being able to connect the ideas from various disciplines and sources makes new discoveries that much more likely.

Burger and Starbird identify the final element of effective thinking as change. They cite that knowledge in any field is more than doubling every five years. That means that not only is new knowledge increasing at an unimaginably rapid rate, but current information is also becoming obsolete just as quickly (about 20% a year).[xxxiv]

It's almost like being on a treadmill that never stops moving. If you don't keep pace with it, you will fall off. In order to keep up, you must accept that change is inevitable and embrace it. Be aware of the changes that are going on all around you. Use all of the quality information around you to help you adapt to the changes you are facing. Be flexible enough to adjust or alter your thinking when new evidence warrants it. Never stop learning and growing.

Key Takeaways:

- If you want to master something complex, you must begin by first mastering the simple things.

- Critical thinkers are always trying to increase not only the breadth, but also the depth of their understanding.

- If you truly want to increase your depth of understanding, you must work to overcome your biases and question your own beliefs in order to make sure they are based on facts. It is only then that you will be open-minded enough to be receptive to learning new information.

- Learning from your mistakes as well as your successes and asking questions are some of the most important things you can do as a critical thinker.

- Embrace change and be a lifelong learner. That is the only way to keep up with our constantly changing world today.

Chapter 6: How To Develop Critical Thinking Skills

In order to be a strong critical thinker, you must start with the simple before you can advance to the complex. Take the time to really understand the basic foundation from which all thinking comes. Break thinking down into its core parts so that you can build from there.

When you use the intellectual traits laid out earlier on a regular basis until they become second nature, you will find that you become a strong critical thinker who can:

- Create clear, precise, important questions
- Collect, analyze, and interpret information related to the topic at hand
- Reach informed, well-thought-out conclusions based on facts and evidence
- Be open-minded and receptive to information from a variety of sources, even when it seems to disprove or disagree with your own ideas and beliefs

- Work well with others to solve complex problems

Develop critical thinking practices

How do we begin to develop our critical thinking skills?

1. **Question your assumptions.** People make assumptions. It's just what we do. Assumptions are ideas we accept as being true without having proof. Our brains have to deal with so much information that in order to be able to process it all, they take some shortcuts. Our assumptions are one of these mental shortcuts. They are the foundation on which we build other things. We have to make sure our beliefs are correct, or all of the other ideas we build from them will be faulty as well. We should frequently go back and reexamine our assumptions for accuracy to be certain they are serving us well as we try to think critically and make educated, informed decisions.

2. **Don't accept information on authority unless you've evaluated and confirmed it**

yourself. Checking every bit of information that comes our way is a daunting task. That would take a tremendous amount of time and energy. Often, we instead decide to assess the value of information based on whether or not we think it came from a reputable, trustworthy source or not. This means we don't check information that we think came from a trustworthy source. The danger lies in what happens when we just assume that anything printed in a book or shown on television must true. We need to trust our instincts, and when we think information sounds questionable, commit to doing a little more research. Ask for more information that supports a particular conclusion, or search for other sources that either prove or disprove that conclusion. Make it a habit, and then, before you know it, you will be able to pick up on when you need to do some more investigating and when the information is actually evidence-based and can be trusted.

3. **Question things.** Not only question assumptions and authority figures, but be

willing to question everything if need be. Questioning is the hallmark feature of critical thinking. If you don't question things, you will never find the answers and truth you seek.

4. **Understand your own biases.** No matter how much we would like to think it, our judgment isn't always objective. We all carry the baggage of our own biases with us. If we don't acknowledge them and work to overcome them, they will weigh us down and cloud our judgment. They will prevent us from looking at information through our critical thinking lens.

5. **Think several steps ahead.** It's simply not enough to try to stay a few steps ahead. Try to think so far ahead that you can imagine all possible outcomes and consequences. This will help guide you through the critical thinking process and prepare you as well as possible for whatever will come your way. You will always encounter surprises that you didn't plan for, but the better prepared you are and the more thought you have put into it

in advance, the more equipped you will be to handle it.

6. **Read a book and embrace all that it has to offer.** Books are powerful things. They can present us with alternative viewpoints and inspire debate, cause us to feel emotions we didn't expect, and teach us things we have never learned before. Books are food for our minds.

7. **Express empathy.** When we can see things through another's eyes, we begin to understand more deeply their feelings, point of view, and motivation. Empathy makes us a stronger critical thinker because it allows us to learn from different perspectives than just our own. And as an added bonus, it just might make us a better person as well.

8. **Explore your options.** Too often we assume that we don't have any options, or at least that our options are very limited. Taking the time to really dig in and explore our options might reveal that we have more, or better, options than we thought. Write them down, work to understand

what the outcomes may be if you choose each one, and really weigh your options before you reach a conclusion or make a decision. You may find that things are not as bad as you thought.

9. **Realize that there are limits to your knowledge and reach out to others who may have wisdom to share.** Our self-esteem might like to think that we are very smart, but the smartest thing we can do is admit that there are others who are smarter than we are in certain areas. The smartest people in the world know that it is impossible to be brilliant in every area and are willing to seek help from others who have knowledge that they don't. There is no shame in acknowledging that. If our goal is to constantly improve and grow, then we should be eager to learn new things from other people.

10. **Never say never, but stand firm when you are justified.** As we discussed earlier, our knowledge is changing at a frantic pace in today's world. Knowledge that we have today could likely be obsolete tomorrow. Roughly 20% of our

information becomes obsolete over the course of a single year. We need to do our due diligence to use our critical thinking skills to analyze information for accuracy today, and defend it when we have facts and evidence to back it up. We should be willing to defend our views and ideas as long as we have evidence to support them. At the same time, we need to keep an open mind, realizing that while our theories are on firm ground right now, there is always the possibility of new information coming to light that could disprove them in the future. With an open mind and strong critical thinking skills, we can be receptive to adjusting our viewpoint when necessary.

11. **Exercise diplomacy.** Recognize that the world is filled with at least as many people who will disagree with you as people who will agree. All too often people get so defensive about their viewpoint that they are offended when anyone dares to disagree with it. They may become angry and even attack those who have a perspective that stands in opposition to their own. That does not serve a critical

thinker well at all. Critical thinkers strive to find the truth and learn new things. They are works in progress who are constantly trying to improve themselves. They seek information that will help them make informed decisions and reach accurate conclusions. The only way that critical thinkers can achieve their goals is to be open and welcoming to the knowledge and viewpoints of others. Gathering information from people of all different ages, backgrounds, and perspectives is crucial.

12. **Learn how to critique information effectively.** This is a skill that is not easy or automatic for people to master. It takes effort and practice to hone the skill. Pay attention to how others critique arguments. Analyze them for strengths and weaknesses. Learn from the mistakes and successes of others and incorporate what you learn into your own critiques.

13. **Assess the method of reasoning used to support an argument or viewpoint.** Examine the logic that people use to reach their conclusions. Decide if they have

taken something specific and stretched it to say that it applies to the entire group (the general) or if they started with something general and broad and then brought it down to the specific. When you understand how they support their conclusions, you can begin to find faults in it or test the theory to see if it stands up to evidence.

Asking questions in different situations

There is an art to asking questions. The way that we ask questions can lead to improved critical thinking. Questions can be asked in a variety of ways, depending upon the desired information we would like to learn.

If your goal is to remember information, you will likely be trying to list, name, identify, or describe things. Committing information to memory can be helped by making connections between the new information you are learning and knowledge you already have. Questions you may want to ask in this situation could be:

- What do we already know about this topic?

- How does what we are learning now fit in with what we already learned earlier?

Trying to understand and interpret information for deeper meaning likely means you will be describing, explaining, or predicting things. Questions that may prove helpful are:

- What does this mean?
- What might the result be if this happened?
- Can you summarize the core ideas?

If you are moving into higher thinking skills and you want to take some information you already know and apply it to a new situation, you will probably be trying to use, demonstrate, hypothesize, implement, or solve things. Some questions that can be used for this purpose are:

- What would happen if this changed?
- How could this be used in a different or new way?
- What is an additional example?

If your purpose is to analyze information, you are breaking it down into smaller pieces so that you can study it more closely. You will be attempting to compare and contrast, organize, and take apart the information. Helpful questions may include:

- How is this piece of information different?
- Why is this fact or evidence important?
- How are these pieces of information alike?
- Can you explain how or why?

When you evaluate information you are deciding if it has merit based on a set of standards. You will be trying to judge, critique, conclude, assess, and explain. Good questions to use for evaluating include:

- Do you agree or disagree with the information? What evidence do you have to support your answer?
- Why is this happening?
- How does this affect other things?

The highest level of thinking is when you are creating. This happens when you take parts of things and combine them together to make new patterns. You will be designing, constructing, planning, and making something new. Questions that may prove helpful for this purpose are:

- What do you think causes this?
- What is another way of looking at this?
- What is a possible solution to this problem?

Key Takeaways:

- The ability to ask clear, precise, important questions is an essential one for strong critical thinkers. They need to question not only new information, but also their own assumptions. How you frame a question can help you to achieve a desired purpose.

- After you have reached well-thought-out, informed conclusions based on facts and evidence, you should be able to stand behind and defend your viewpoint, but always be open-minded to the possibility that new information may come along that makes it necessary for you to change or adjust your point of view.

- Critical thinkers understand the importance of being open and receptive to listening and considering perspectives that differ from their own. They are empathetic and do not attack others just because they disagree.

- Critical thinkers realize that it is humanly impossible to be an expert in all areas. They are willing and eager to learn from others who have knowledge they don't. They know the goal is to always learn new things and work to improve themselves.

Chapter 7: Barriers to Critical Thinking

Critical thinking is the ability to think about an issue and reach an objective, informed conclusion based on facts and evidence without being unduly influenced by personal biases and interests, unsubstantiated assumptions, or the unproven opinions of others. We have all likely rushed to judgement about a person or situation or made a hasty decision without taking the time to gather all of the facts and come to regret it later. Critical thinking is designed to help us avoid that feeling of regret. This chapter will discuss the human tendencies and other barriers that may stand in our way and prevent us from thinking critically. If we can acknowledge and understand these barriers, we will be taking a big step toward overcoming them.

Egocentrism

Egocentrism is our tendency to make everything about us and think that we are more important than other people. Thinking about our wants, needs, and the way we believe others perceive us consumes most of our thoughts throughout the day. While it is perfectly normal to direct the majority of our attention to our own personal interests, it isn't necessarily helpful when we are trying to think objectively.

For example, there may be times when we are asked to give our opinions of others. It can be hard to overcome our own egocentric views in order to give an honest, objective response. We may be thinking of how we will be affected in the long run from what we say—like they may get a raise when we won't, or they may get closer to one of our good friends. We may be thinking of how they slighted us one time and allow it to overshadow other evidence of their character. In any case, our own personal feelings and interests may be a barrier to us giving a thoughtful, objective assessment and using our critical thinking skills.

When we can't remove our personal interests from the equation and see things from other people's perspectives, our egocentrism is standing in the way of our ability to think critically. While egocentrism lessens in most people once they reach adulthood, it never completely leaves us. It is present in varying degrees in each person at every stage of life and is something we must acknowledge and fight to overcome.

There is scientific evidence to back this up as well. A research study conducted by Baron and Hanna tested 152 participants between the ages of 18 and 25 to see if there was a connection between depression and egocentrism. They reported that people suffering from depression display higher levels of egocentrism than those who don't.[xxxv]

Surtees and Apperley conducted a study asking adults to judge the number of dots they saw and the number of dots an avatar on the computer saw. The findings showed that the adults made errors due to their egocentric view in assuming that the avatar would have the same perspective and view that they did. They found that egocentric thoughts are even more likely when people make quick judgments. As we know, rushing to judgment without taking into account a variety of perspectives goes against the skills strong critical thinkers exhibit.[xxxvi]

Human nature doesn't automatically give a lot of attention and weight to the thoughts and feelings of others. We do not always recognize that our own point of view is limited and that we can learn from others' points of view. These are things we have to work at and practice. We tend to believe we have everything figured out and don't realize how subjectively we actually view the world. Acknowledging our natural egocentric tendencies and constantly working to overcome them is a great place to start in our quest to develop and improve our critical thinking skills.[xxxvii]

Sociocentrism

Not only do we think that we are more important than others, but we extend that line of thought to the people we are closest to—our own social group. It is human nature to think that our social group is superior to and correct more often than other social groups. This is a form of group bias. Group bias is when a group collectively holds their own mutual self-interest in higher regard than that of other groups around them. It is when you give greater weight to your own group's goals than you do to others. When group bias is at work, you are likely to forgive the members of your group when they make a mistake more readily than you are willing to accept the same behaviors and mistakes from others outside of your group.

People often exhibit herd instinct when it comes to their social group. Herd instinct is when you are willing to forego critical thinking in order to blindly follow your group in the hopes of fitting in. Human nature means that no one wants to feel like an outcast, so it is easy to fall into the trap of allowing the social group to influence your decisions at the expense of critical thinking. People are often willing to put the group's needs, wants, and beliefs above everything else. This is sociocentrism at its worst.[xxxviii]

Inconsistencies

The inconsistency fallacy is when an argument contains two different ideas that stand in direct contradiction to each other. We should periodically check on our beliefs to be certain they are still based on facts and evidence. We should also check for consistency. Consistency among beliefs is key in critical thinking. If we have beliefs that are contradictory to one another, that means it is impossible for them both to be true.

One or both of them are definitely false. This requires further analysis on our part for clarification. Believing two ideas that contradict one another is a logical inconsistency.

Another kind of inconsistency happens when our actions don't match up with what we say we believe. This is called a practical inconsistency. It is when we say one thing, but do another. For example, if I say being on time is important and I always show up late for everything, I am being practically inconsistent because my words and actions are in direct contradiction with one another.

Stubbornness

Another barrier to critical thinking is stubbornness. While it is important to hold onto our ideas and beliefs when they are rooted in fact and supported by evidence, it is not beneficial to cling to ideas that are not. Stubbornness is when we continue to defend and subscribe to our beliefs, even when there is evidence to refute them. When we are presented with new information, we need to analyze its relevance and accuracy. Once we have carefully done that using our critical thinking skills, we must be open-minded enough to be willing to let go of, or modify, our previously held beliefs, if the evidence warrants it.

Prejudice

Our critical thinking skills are greatly hindered by our bias and prejudice. We all know that being prejudiced or biased against others is morally wrong. I would even wager to say that the majority of people probably think they are not biased or prejudiced, but we are all to varying degrees. The sooner we accept and acknowledge that fact, the sooner we can commit to increasing our awareness of our personal biases and work toward overcoming them.

Prejudices and biases are usually subtle, and can sneak up on us if we aren't cognizant of them. We are all a product of our culture and traditions, which are a major influence on the way we see the world. This does not make us bad people, it makes us human. Everything we have experienced in our lives makes us who we are and helps to form our thoughts and opinions.

Our experiences form the lens through which we look at ourselves and others. It leaves us exposed to being subjective when through critical thinking, objectivity is our goal. Being aware of our personal biases and prejudices are our first line of defense in combatting them.

Fear

Our thoughts and beliefs are a source of comfort for us. They create our comfort zone—the place where we feel safe, unjudged, and among friends. Anything that makes us question our beliefs sort of shakes us to our core and makes us feel uneasy, or even afraid. Too often, people would rather "not know," so they avoid asking questions or seriously listening to and considering points of view that are different from their own out of fear that they will be forced to change their minds. Fear hinders our ability to be strong critical thinkers. Stepping out of our comfort zone is necessary in critical thinking.

Laziness

Laziness is another barrier to critical thinking. Critical thinking takes time and energy. It requires effort and commitment on our part. I never claimed that critical thinking would be easy, but it will be worth it. Critical thinking happens with hard work. If we want to be critical thinkers, we must be willing to be active participants in our own learning. It requires us to collect information, analyze it, consider multiple perspectives, and be ready to modify or abandon our ideas in the face of new evidence, if warranted. It is an unrelenting commitment to seek the truth and not give up until we find it. It is impossible to be lazy and be a critical thinker.

People make common errors in judgment that stand in the way of them exercising their critical skills. Five of these thinking errors are:

- "It's true because *I* believe it." This is egocentrism at work in its purest form.
- "It's true because *we* believe it." This is a display of sociocentrism.
- "It's true because I want to believe it." This is the human nature to not want to have to admit when we have made a mistake.
- "It's true because I have always believed it." Our long-held beliefs are a source of comfort for us, and it can be scary to step out of our comfort zone.

- "It's true because it is in my own personal interest to believe it." This is another example of egocentric thought.[xxxix]

There are additional barriers to critical thinking, which include:

- peer pressure
- blaming others
- being defensive
- resistance to change
- ignorance
- fear of being wrong
- pride
- close-mindedness
- greed
- denial
- apathy
- superstition
- poor communication skills

No matter what barrier is preventing us from reaching our full potential as a critical thinker, they all have something in common. When these barriers are active in our lives, we have no way to control the impacts they will make. The barriers put us in a reactive position, whereas a critical thinker is more proactive. A critical thinker is in the driver's seat, choosing how they will act. Their evaluation of information allows them to correctly judge potential consequences, and guides them to reach an informed and accurate conclusion. A person who is at the mercy of these barriers is in the passenger's seat and can only buckle up, hold on, and hope for the best.

Now it is time to do a little self-reflection. Please take a moment to consider the following questions:

- Why is it beneficial to develop critical thinking skills? Is it necessary?
- What rewards and challenges can I expect?
- Am I willing to put in the necessary time and effort? Is it something I am ready to commit to?
- Am I ready to start combatting the barriers to critical thinking so that I can overcome them?
- Do I realize that this is a lifelong process, and that I will always be a work in

progress constantly trying to improve my skills?
- What steps do I need to take to begin developing my critical thinking skills?
- Will I be able to communicate with people who aren't critical thinkers, and whose barriers prevent them from participating in a respectful and meaningful discussion? Or should I not even try to communicate with them?
- How should I react when a lack of critical thinking skills is evident in my friends and family, colleagues, the media, and other settings?

Critical thinking skills are invaluable tools for everyone to have. Acknowledging and working to overcome the barriers to critical thinking will allow you to have better relationships with others, be a leader, be better equipped to achieve your personal and professional goals, make informed decisions, and experience a sense of greater purpose and satisfaction in your life. Overcoming these barriers can help to remove the roadblocks to your overall happiness.

Key Takeaways:

- Developing critical thinking skills is a lifelong process that takes time and effort as you constantly strive to improve your skills.

- There are many barriers that can prevent you from reaching your full potential as a critical thinker. The first step to overcoming them is acknowledging their existence and making the effort to better understand them.

- Barriers to critical thinking have the potential to exist in all of us at all stages of our lives. They can manifest quietly without us even realizing it, if we aren't careful.

- When we allow the barriers to overpower our thinking, we are robbing ourselves of the chance to be a proactive participant in reaching quality, objective, informed conclusions.

- Developing critical thinking skills can have many far-reaching positive effects on our lives. They are beneficial to everyone.

Chapter 8: On Ethics and Impartiality

Critical thinking skills are key if we want to be certain we are thinking for ourselves and making informed decisions and conclusions about the information we learn. This is why it is important for us to begin teaching critical thinking skills as soon as possible. Making sure that we introduce and begin practicing these skills in elementary school will only serve to benefit students throughout their lives. Having strong critical thinking skills is the best way to overcome any attempts at indoctrination.

Avoiding Indoctrination

Indoctrination is when ideas are taught expressly from one point of view. The expectation is that the ideas will be unconditionally accepted without critical examination or thought. Children begin to learn what is ethical and morally right from a very early age. The sooner that we can begin to equip them with critical thinking skills, the better prepared they will be to make moral and ethical judgments that will shape their characters throughout their lifetimes.

If we attempt to teach children what types of behavior are morally right and wrong without exposing them to the critical thinking skills that they can use to analyze them, we are opening them up to falling prey to the barriers to critical thinking skewing their judgment and keeping them from a deeper understanding of morals and ethics. This is true not only of children, but also to people of any age who lack the skills necessary to think critically.

Morals and ethics are tricky to teach and learn because while it seems that all people could agree on a set standard for moral behavior, the reality is that the world is not so black and white. There are a lot of gray areas where one correct answer is not clear, or does not even exist. This is why that more often than not people disagree about what constitutes moral and ethical behavior in a specific situation. There tends to be more agreement on broad general principles.

For example, the vast majority of people would agree that stealing is morally wrong. That is a broad, general principle. But if people are presented with a specific situation about someone who stole because they could not provide food for their family, there would be a lot more disagreement over whether it would or would not be morally appropriate for them to steal in that specific circumstance.

People can only be expected to do what is morally right and ethical if they know what that is. If they mistake their sense of what is ethical for their own egocentric wants and needs, or the sociocentric views they share with their social group, they will not be able to make decisions about what is ethical. The best way to avoid allowing personal interests to cloud moral judgment is to use critical thinking skills to analyze situations carefully and reach objective, informed conclusions. When people lack critical thinking skills, it is easy for others to pass along their own biases, prejudices, and close-mindedness to them either inadvertently or intentionally. Then they will be indoctrinated to see things as being morally right or wrong from only one perspective, without being able to question them and make an informed decision for themselves. The best way to guard against this happening is to develop strong critical thinking skills and practice using them to analyze a variety of situations from various perspectives to determine if morals and ethics are being followed or abandoned.

Stay impartial

We might think that we are able to stay impartial in any given situation, but staying impartial isn't nearly as easy as we think. Take the media, for example. Most media sources profess to impartially deliver the news, and I genuinely believe that most of them want to. But there is an underlying risk, a sort of a catch-22, that can be hard to escape. The simple fact is that words have power. They carry with them a literal meaning, but also a connotation. A connotation is a feeling that words can invoke in people. When the media reports information they must be very careful about their word selection, because the words that they choose to use will create a feeling in others whether that is their intention or not.

It is human nature for people to want to collect information that supports their ideas and point of view so they will naturally be drawn to read or watch media outlets that choose words with connotations they like and agree with. When those media outlets analyze who composes the largest part of their reading or viewing audience, they continue to make word selections in their delivery of information that will keep the support of their audience. I am not saying that they are not being truthful in their reporting at all. Many of them may not even fully recognize the weight their word choice carries. They just become a part of a catch-22, which is a dilemma that becomes a cycle they can't escape from because they depend on attracting an audience in order to stay in business. Even those with the very best intentions of staying impartial may find it difficult to remain so in every situation.

Adolf Hitler was someone in history who knew how difficult it is for people to remain impartial. He was very skilled at understanding how to persuade people to his way of thinking. He knew that in order to get his message across in such a way that countless people would follow it, he had to keep his message short. Hitler understood that presenting a message as a short slogan was far preferable to an argument. Presenting his views as an argument would open them up to debate, and he wanted to avoid that at all costs. Instead, a well-thought-out slogan that appealed to his audience (he knew them very well) and played upon their emotions was infinitely more effective.

It was easier for them to remember and harder for anyone to argue against. Thus, many people were far more willing to shed their impartiality and critical thinking abilities in order to follow Hitler than they probably ever imagined they would be. We all know the horrible consequences that followed...

The only hope we have for remaining impartial is to commit to exercising and constantly improving our critical thinking skills. We have to be aware of our own personal biases and prejudices that stand in the way of thinking critically, and we must work every day to overcome them. Otherwise, it is easy to get swept up by our own personal interests and emotions, rather than striving to be objective and analyze information to help uncover the truth we desire.

Key Takeaways:

- Impartiality is difficult to achieve. It requires a commitment to finding the truth, no matter the source. It takes effort and great analysis on our part.

- In order to do what is ethical and morally right, we must know what that is. This requires critical thinking skills in order to make sound moral judgments.

- People lacking in critical thinking skills may be easily indoctrinated by others, inadvertently or intentionally, and be cheated from reaching their own conclusions about what is morally right or wrong.

- It can be easy to confuse one's egocentric wants and needs or the sociocentric views of one's social group with a sense of what is ethical.

Conclusion

Critical thinking is the desire to seek the truth by analyzing information from a variety of points of view in the hopes of reaching objective, informed conclusions. In this book, we went through the benefits of critical thinking, the obstacles that stand between you and your critical thinking skills, and we saw the ugly damage a lack of critical thinking can cause. All that remains for you to do now is practice, practice, practice. If available information was the answer, all of us would be billionaires, have perfect bodies, and be excellent chefs. Why are we not? Because it's not information that makes things happen, but action.

What can you do to start becoming a better critical thinker in practice? Critical thinkers know that they do not have all the answers and they are willing to reach out to others who have knowledge they do not. They are willing to question everything, including themselves and their ideas, to be certain that the information they are receiving is based on facts and evidence.

This is a skill we have to be willing to work for, critical thinking does not come naturally to us. Our brains are lazy and usually seek the easiest, shortest answer by default. Accept that you are a work in progress and strive to improve and further develop your skills. Be willing to give equal weight and consideration to all viewpoints, even those which stand in stark contrast to your own in an effort to learn something new.

Have confidence in your beliefs, if you have taken the time to carefully analyze them and made sure they are supported by evidence. But also put a limit to that confidence. Don't stubbornly hold on to those beliefs at all costs. Recognize how quickly knowledge can become obsolete. When you are presented with new facts and evidence that disputes you beliefs, stay open-minded and willing to modify them, if that's the case.

Strong critical thinkers aren't interested in taking the easy way out. They are interested in achieving results. They realize that critical thinking skills can positively impact all areas of their lives. From stronger relationships to improved leadership attributes and everything in between, critical thinking can offer benefits to everyone as long as they are willing to put in the work. Because, after all, "We reap what we sow."

If you are willing to make the effort to develop your critical thinking skills, you just might find that you can achieve goals and have a greater sense of happiness and satisfaction in life beyond what you ever imagined possible.

Good luck!

Steve

Reference

Baron, P. Hanna, J. Egocentrism and depressive symptomatology in young adults. Social Behavior and Personality. 18 (2): 279–285. doi:10.2224/sbp.1990.18.2.279. 1990.

Burger, Edward B. Starbird, Michael. Five Elements Of Effective Thinking. Princeton University Press. 2012.

Cherry, Kendra. Concrete Operational Stage of Cognitive Development. Very Well. 2018. https://www.verywell.com/concrete-operational-stage-of-cognitive-development-2795458

Cherry, Kendra. Formal Operational Stage of Cognitive Development. Very Well. 2018. https://www.verywell.com/formal-operational-stage-of-cognitive-development-2795459

Cherry, Kendra. Preoperational Stage of Cognitive Development. Very Well. 2018. https://www.verywell.com/preoperational-stage-of-cognitive-development-2795461

Cherry, Kendra. What Happens During the Sensorimotor Stage of Cognitive Development? Very Well. 2018. https://www.verywell.com/sensorimotor-stage-of-cognitive-development-2795462

Elder, Linda. Paul, Richard. The Analysis & Assessment of Thinking. Critical Thinking. 2017. http://www.criticalthinking.org/pages/the-analysis-amp-assessment-of-thinking/497

Elder, Linda. Paul, Richard. Universal Intellectual Standards. Critical Thinking. 2017. http://www.criticalthinking.org/pages/universal-intellectual-standards/527

Frank, T. What is Critical Thinking? - Definition, Skills & Meaning. Study. 2018.

http://study.com/academy/lesson/what-is-critical-thinking-definition-skills-meaning.html

Gilkey, Roderick. Caceda, Ricardo. Kilts, Clinton When Emotional Reasoning Trumps IQ. Harvard Business Review. 2010.
https://hbr.org/2010/09/when-emotional-reasoning-trumps-iq

Insight Assessment. Expert Consensus on Critical Thinking. Insight Assessment. 2018.
https://www.insightassessment.com/Resources/Importance-of-Critical-Thinking/Expert-Consensus-on-Critical-Thinking

Loewenstein, G., O'Donoghue, T., & Rabin, M. Projection bias in predicting future utility. Quarterly Journal of Economics, 118(4), 1209-1248. 2003.

McLeod, Saul. Jean Piaget. Simply Psychology. 2015.
https://www.simplypsychology.org/piaget.html

Nickerson, R. S. Confirmation bias: A ubiquitous phenomenon in many guises. Review of General Psychology, 2, 175-220. 1998.

O'Reilly, Kim. PhD. Why Critical Thinking Is So Important. Intercultural Solutions. 2008.
https://www.interculturalsolutions.net/why-critical-thinking-is-so-important/

Picture I. Thinking, Critical. Critical Thinking: Where to Begin. Critical Thinking. 2017.
http://www.criticalthinking.org/pages/critical-thinking-where-to-begin/796

Russel, Robert. What Are Four Barriers to Critical Thinking? Classroom. 2018.
http://classroom.synonym.com/four-barriers-critical-thinking-8427849.html

Serva, Christine. Common Barriers to Critical Thinking. Study. 2018.
http://study.com/academy/lesson/common-barriers-to-critical-thinking.html